beth hillel
congregation
LIBRARY
3220 big tree lane
Wilmette, Illinois 60091

presented by

_____

_____

in memory of / honor of

_____

_____

THE JEWISH HOLIDAY

DO - BOOK

Written by Lois Englander

Gail Kansky

and Judy Sacks

with Jay Englander

Illustrated by Gail Kansky

DEDICATION

We dedicate this book to our families for their encouragement and patience and for sharing our desire to enrich the lives of Jewish children.

Copyright © 1976 by Gail Kansky, Lois Englander and Judy Sacks

All rights reserved including the right of

reproduction in any form.

Library of Congress Catalog Card No.: 76-55506

SBN: 0-8197-0451-2

Permission to copy any part of this book must be obtained from:

BLOCH PUBLISHING COMPANY, INC.

915 Broadway

New York, New York 10010

TABLE OF CONTENTS

SHABBAT......................11

ROSH HASHANA AND YOM KIPPUR........32

SUCCOT AND SIMCHAT TORAH...........53

CHANUKAH......................73

PURIM......................95

TU B'SHVAT......................115

PASSOVER......................134

SHAVUOT......................156

INTRODUCTION

Children learn by hearing, seeing, tasting, and even smelling... but they remember by doing. Thus, The Jewish Holiday Do-Book was born.

This book is designed for children from 3 to 103. Holiday crafts, songs, dances, games, and recipes are presented in an easy-to-follow format. Careful attention has been given to the material to make it attractive and inviting for use both by children and adults. It is a welcome addition to the home, the Temple, and the school library.

We encourage the child to expand upon or vary each activity according to his or her own sense of creativity...to discover what fun it is to "do-it" with the help of The Jewish Holiday Do-Book!

The Authors

SAFETY TIPS FOR ALL CRAFT ACTIVITIES

1. Every creative endeavor for a child is bound to make things messy, so always add to your materials one extra...patience. The excitement, manual skill improvements, and re-enforcement of the upcoming holiday will be well worth the messiness! Cleaning up is another skill that should be included in the activity for the child.

2. An adult should be present for all activities where the child may need supervision. Those activities marked for pre-schoolers are intended to be done with close supervision for safety as well as to limit frustration on the part of the youngster.

3. Assemble all craft materials before the activity begins and read all the instructions carefully before starting.

4. Scissors should always be carried closed. When they are not in use, put them away. Knives, like scissors, should be safely put away when not needed.

5. To help prevent accidents, do not leave objects on the floor.

6. Never pour melted wax into the sink. Extra wax should be poured into a container and allowed to cool and harden. Wax can be re-melted and used again.

7. Let the child be as creative as he pleases, even if it means that his craft does not look like the one pictured. Encourage his own ideas to add to or differ from the activities found in this book.

MUSIC

We have included original songs as well as old folk tunes with new words in order to retain the creative flavor of this book. The traditional and more familiar songs have been listed by their respective holiday and may be found in the following books and records located in libraries and book stores:

Books:

1. Heritage of Jewish Music, (HJM), by Judith K. Eisenstein (New York: U.A.H.C.), 1973.
2. More of the Songs We Sing, (MSWS), selected and edited by Harry Coopersmith (New York: United Synagogue Commission on Jewish Education), 1971.
3. The New Jewish Song Book, (NJSB), compiled and edited by Harry Coopersmith (New York: Behrman House, Inc.), 1965.
4. Songs of Childhood, (SoC), by Judith Eistenstein and Freda Prensky (New York: United Synagogue Commission on Jewish Education), 1955.
5. The Songs We Sing, (SWS), selected and edited by Harry Coopersmith (New York: United Synagogue Commission on Jewish Education), 1950.

Records:

1. Chanukah Song Parade, (CSP), by Gladys Gewirtz and Eve Lippman, distributed by The House of Menorah Inc. New York.

2. Menorah's Little Seder and Seder Sing Along, (SSA), Menorah Records, Inc.

3. Purim Song Parade, (PSP), directed by Albert H. Arkus, distributed by Menorah Records.

4. Edge of Freedom, (EOF), by Bell Records, published by Aim Records (EM)

5. Music Makers, (MM), by Camp Fire Girls, Inc.

DANCES

New dances with original choreography are included in this book. The traditional and well-established dances, already a part of the Jewish culture, are found in the sources listed below:

1. Dances for Jewish Festivals by D'vora Lapson, (New York: Jewish Education Commission).

2. Ha-Rikud - The Jewish Dance (paperback) by Fred Berk, (New York: Union of American Hebrew Congregations), 1975.

3. Jewish Folk Dance Book by Delkova-Berk, (New York: Jewish Education Commission).

4. Jewish Holiday Dances by Corine Cochem, (New York: Behrman House, Inc.), 1948.

RECIPES

The simple recipes found on the following pages have easy-to-read directions. Each section features tasty treats for that special holiday. Proper supervision is stressed whenever the stove or oven is being used.

Important Rules to Follow

1. Wash hands carefully.
2. Put on a clean apron.
3. Read each recipe twice.
4. Lay out all the ingredients. Be sure to have everything you need before you begin.
5. Have a sponge ready to wipe up spills.
6. Use a pot holder for handling hot pots and pans.
7. Be sure to grease pans when necessary.
8. Always have an adult set the oven to the correct temperature or supervise this procedure.
9. Wash all the dishes, pots, and pans.
10. Shut off the oven with supervision.
11. Leave everything just as you found it.

SYMBOLS

T.	tablespoon	pt.	pint
t.	teaspoon	oz.	ounce
c.	cup	qt.	quart
		lb.	pound

MATERIALS

Tablespoon   beater   pan

teaspoon   cup measure   cookie sheet

spatula   bowl

EQUIVALENTS

3 teaspoons are the same as 1 tablespoon

4 tablespoons are the same as 1/4 cup or 2 ounces

2 cups are the same as 1 pint or 16 ounces

1/4 pound butter is the same as 1/2 cup

1 pound is the same as 2 cups

4 cups sifted flour are the same as 1 pound

CLAY CANDLE HOLDERS

You will need:

Playing dough or any self-hardening clay

pencil

lacquer

acrylic paint

Large cookie molds (optional)

sponge

water

---

1. Shape clay free hand or with molds to desired shape. Use pencil for textures and design.

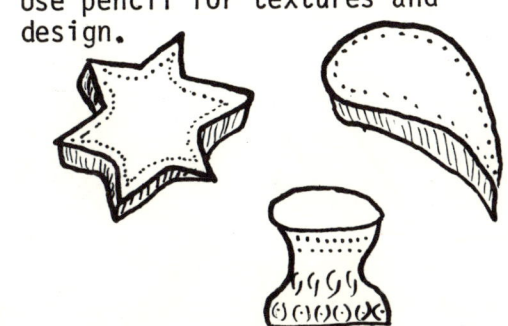

2. Insert pencil (or a candle) in shape and wiggle until hole is enlarged.

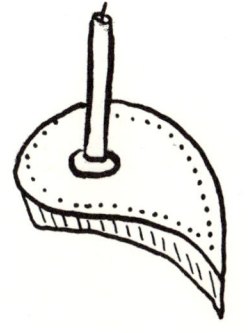

---

3. Let dry thoroughly. When dry, smooth with moist sponge. Then paint with acrylics.

4. After paint is dry (about 20 minutes), apply coat of lacquer to protect the holder.

11

SIMPLE CHALLE COVER

You will need:

A piece of solid colored fabric

Things to decorate it with such as:

felt-tip pens	bits of colored felt
sparkles	embroidery thread and needles
crayons	paste

1. Take a few minutes to "plan out" your design. Decide whether to decorate the border of your fabric, the center, or both.

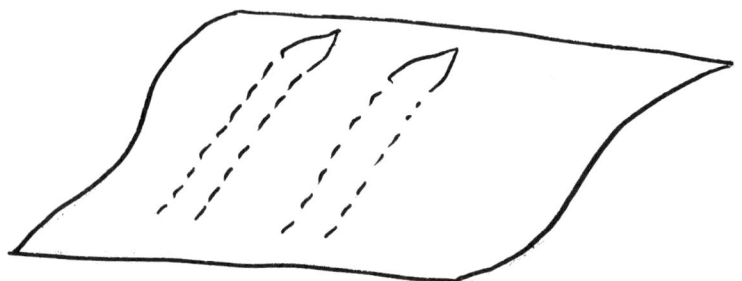

2. Use the supplies in different combinations to decorate your Challe Cover.

Pre-School Up

HAVDALAH CANDLE

The Havdalah candle must have more than one wick and should resemble a torch. It may be of one or more colors, twisted or braided. We have chosen the simplest method so that the pre-schooler can make his own Havdalah candle. More difficult ways may be tried for the older child.

You will need:

   Two long and narrow candles of different colors

   Stove and pot

---

1. Boil some water on a stove and hold the candles over the pot in the steam until they are flexible. (For a younger child, we suggest placing the candles in the top half of a double boiler, then, when flexible, have the adult hold one end, while the child twists.)

---

2. Now twist (or braid) the candles together. Let harden in air.

---

3. (Optional): After the twisted or braided candle has hardened, dip it in some melted wax. The result will be a soft, glazed effect.

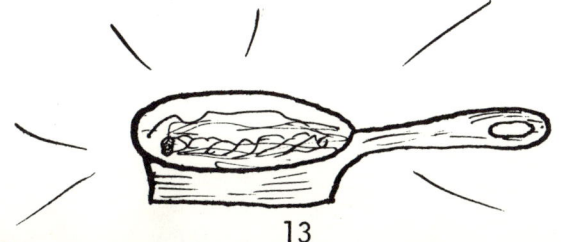

SALT AND PEPPER SHAKERS

You will need:

    2 plastic prescription bottles with caps
    acrylic paints
    large needle
    lacquer

---

1. Pierce holes in tops of bottle caps with large needle.

---

2. Decorate bottles with acrylic paints.

---

3. Coat with lacquer when dry.

ETERNAL LIGHT

You will need:

    Yahrzeit candle
    tin can with one end intact
    water
    freezer
    hammer

    nail
    paper
    pencil
    wire

---

1. Wash your can thoroughly and remove all paper and glue from outside.

2. Fill the can with water and place in freezer until water has turned to solid ice.

---

2. Draw a design on a piece of paper. Make sure the design will fit on the tin can.

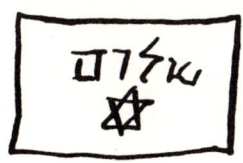

4. Place the paper on top of the ice filled can and, using the hammer and nail, punch holes in the can to outline your design. Also punch holes 1/4" from the top to attach the wire.

---

5. Attach wire to the top of the can making sure the ends are even and will balance the can. Then twist the ends of the wires tightly into a hook.

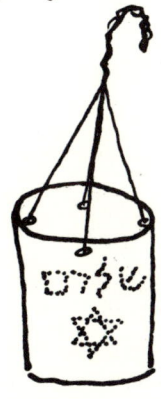

6. Place the candle in the can and suspend it from up high. Light your own eternal light (Ner Tamid) at times of prayer in your own home. If you desire to paint outside of can, make sure paint is heat resistant.

CREPE PAPER CLAY HORSERADISH HOLDER

You will need:

One fold crepe paper (clay will be much lighter so we recommend darker shades)
1 tablespoon salt
1 cup flour (approx.)

water
small tin can
large mixing bowl
varnish or shellac

---

1. Cut crepe paper into tiny, tiny pieces and place in large mixing bowl.

2. Add enough water to cover paper and let it soak for about 15 minutes until it is soft. Then drain off excess water.

3. Add salt to flour, then add dry mix to paper mix...enough to make the dough stiff. Knead the two mixtures together well.

4. Cover tin can with about 3/4" layer of crepe paper clay. Press it down firmly around can.

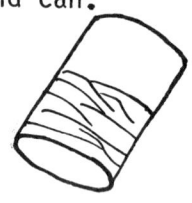

---

5. Set horseradish holder in a warm place for about two days until it is completely hardened and dry. Then give it two coats of varnish or shellac. Paint may be applied before varnishing.

Pre-School
Up

SHABBAT CANDLESTICKS

You will need:

    two cardboard tubes   paints or felt tip pens
    two small paper plates   or crayons
    glue   scissors
                                                   small piece of paper

---

1. Cut four small slits with the scissors on one end of each tube. Bend the slits out.

2. Glue the bent slits to the middle of the paper plate.

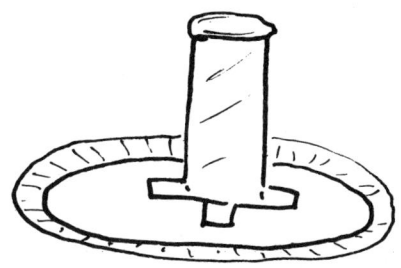

---

3. Color the plate and even the candle if you wish!

4. Cut a small piece of paper in the shape of a flame.

---

5. Color the flame a hot color.

6. Glue the flame inside the tube.

SABBATH'S QUEEN
(a 3-part round)

Lyrics: Gail Kansky
Music: Kum Bachur Atzel
(Jewish Folk Song)

Sab-bath's here a-gain, the last day of the week.

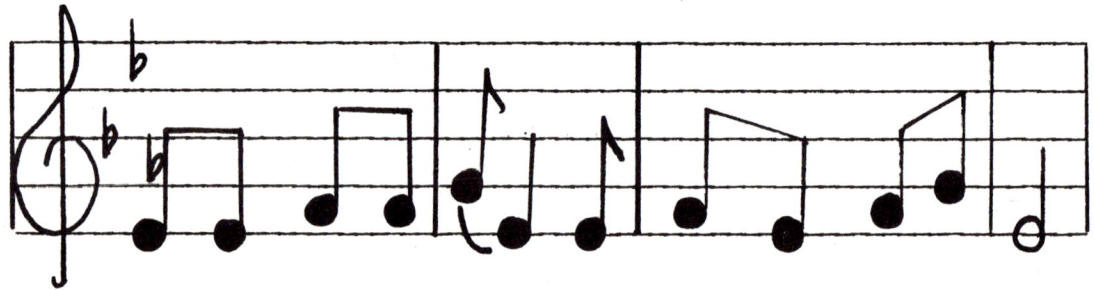
Can-dles wine and chale, God's bles-sings do we seek!

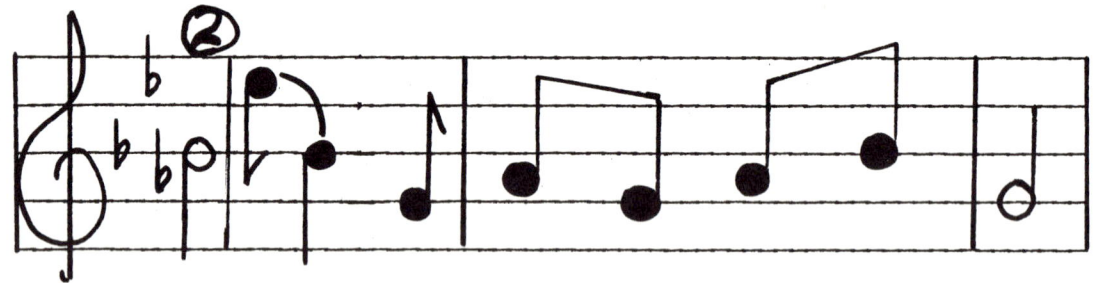
Sing! Sing! To wel-come Sab-bath's Queen.

Sing! Sing! To wel-come Sab-bath's Queen.

18

Refrain

In the glow of Sab-bath can-dles Mo-ther says the prayer.

Sweet as hon-ey Bright and shi-ning Sab-bath's Queen is fair.

© Gail Kansky 1976

SABBATH DANCE

Music: Sabbath's Queen

For this dance start by making two lines so that each child has a partner. (See below if there is an uneven number of dancers.) Face your partner and take one large step backward. The first child in each line make Couple #1.

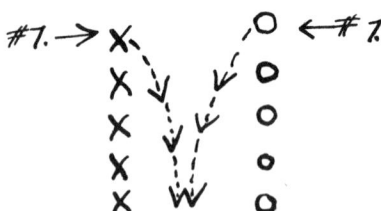

STEP I. <u>Only</u> Couple #1 join both hands and slide down through the center of the two lines for 8 counts and then back for 8 counts. All the other couples are facing each other and clap for 16 counts.

STEP II. Once Couple #1 has returned to the head of the line, everyone turns around in place, 4 counts to the right, and 4 counts to the left. Hands are held high above head and clap in time to the music.

STEP III. Couple #1 each lead <u>their own line</u> around as in the picture below. The step is a small running step, hands clasped behind the back. Follow your own leader around for 8 counts. Then when Couple #1 have reached center back, they make an arch and everyone else grabs his partner's hand and runs through the arch. When everyone has run through, we have a new Couple #1 and we're ready to start again.

If there are an uneven number of dancers, one person should have a tambourene and should sing the song.

DAY OF REST

Music by Jay Englander
Words by Gail Kansky

It's my fav'rite time it's my fav'rite day. We will dress for Temple where we will pray.
There is time to pray, There is time to play. Weekly works behind us. Our hearts are gay.
Light the candles, say the blessings.
Peace and love we pray that Sabbath brings.

© Gail Kansky, Jay Englander 1976

ADDITIONAL SONGS FOR SHABBAT

TITLE	SOURCES
"Hiney Ma Tov"	SWS, NJSB, MSWS
"N'ran'na"	SWS, NJSB, MSWS
"Yom Ze L'Yisroel"	SWS
"V'taher Libenu"	SWS, NJSB, MSWS
"Hin'ni Muhan"	SWS, MSWS
"Shabbat Sholom"	SWS, NJSB, MSWS
"Shiru Ladonoi"	SWS, NJSB
"Yo Ribon Olom"	SWS
"Tzur Mishelo"	SWS, MSWS
"Shir Hama'los"	SWS, NJSB
"Sholom Alehem"	SWS, NJSB, MSWS
"Sabbath Eve"	SWS
"V'Shomru"	SWS, MSWS
"Sim Sholom"	SWS
"En Kelohenu"	SWS, NJSB
"Adon Olom"	SWS, NJSB
"Shavu'a Tov"	SWS, NJSB
"Shalom Haverim"	NJSB, MSWS
"Yis'm'chu"	MSWS
"Shabbat Hamalka"	SWS, NJSB, MSWS

WHAT IS MISSING?

Name the objects found on a holiday table. Name them again leaving out one of the objects. The children must guess the missing object.

>Example: On the Shabbat table there is a kiddush cup, candles, prayer book and tablecloth. Repeat the items: Kiddush cup, candles, and prayer book.
>
>Answer: Tablecloth

I AM SHABBAT

The children sit in a circle. The leader says "candle." The children must respond with a word match. The child who has the right answer claps his hands and gives the word. The other children clap twice if the answer is correct, tap floor if it is incorrect.

>Example: Leader says "candle."
>Child claps and says "Menorah". Other children respond by clapping twice.

WHO HAS THE CANDLE?

You will need:

　　Chair
　　Candle

A child sits in a chair with his back to the other children. A candle is placed on the floor under the chair. A player quietly tiptoes up to the candle and takes it back to his place. The child in the chair has three guesses to name the child with the candle.

ADD A LETTER

The object of this game is to make a word as fast as you can. A child gives a letter, the next child adds a letter. Each child in turn adds a letter until a word is made. A point is given for each word.

　　　　Example: Child one says "h"
　　　　　　　　 Child two says "a"
　　　　　　　　 Child three says "t", has made the
　　　　　　　　 word "hat" and gets the point

CHALLE

You will need:

    4 cups flour   2 T. sugar
    1 packet of yeast   2 T. vegetable oil
    1 1/4 cups warm water   1 T. salt
    2 eggs   bowl which has been
                                                      lightly greased
                                                        towel

In a small dish dissolve the yeast in 1/4 c. warm water.

In a large bowl pour the 4 c. flour and make a "hole" in the center.

Add ingredients <u>in this order</u>, pouring them into the "hole":

    1 c. water, dissolved yeast, eggs, sugar, oil, salt

Mix well with a spoon. Place on the table and knead well for about 5-10 minutes.

Put the dough in a bowl that has been lightly greased and cover with a towel. Let the dough rise for 2 hours.

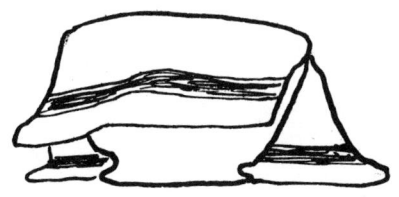

CHALLE (continued)

After the dough has risen knead it again and break it into 3 pieces to braid.

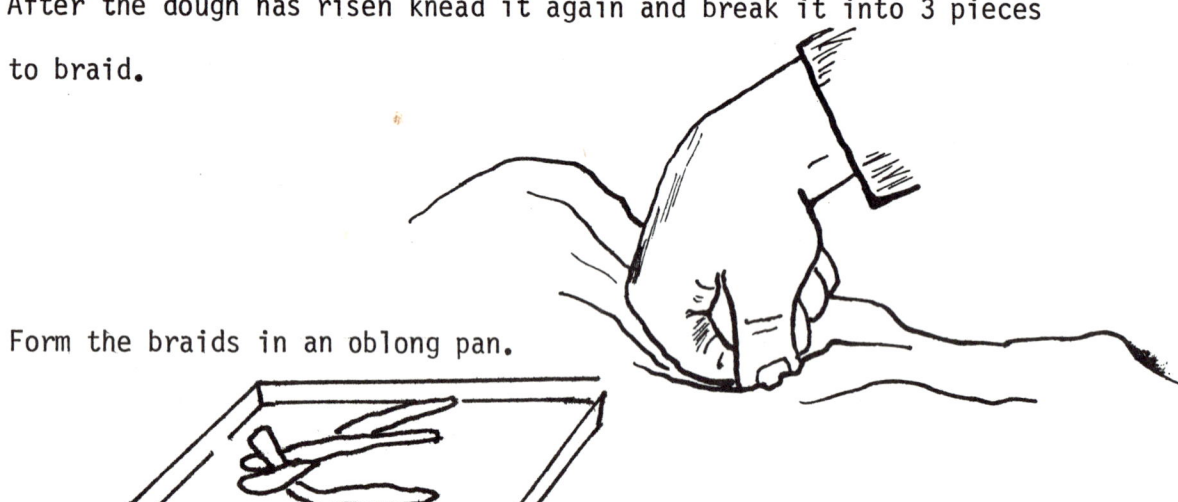

Form the braids in an oblong pan.

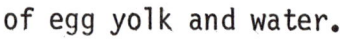

Let it rise for another 25 minutes. Then brush the top with a mixture of egg yolk and water.

Set the oven at 350° and bake for 1 hour.

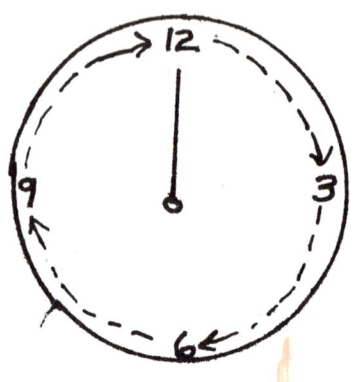

CHICKEN SOUP

You will need:

- 5 lb. chicken
- 2 quarts water
- 1 large onion
- 4 carrots
- 4 carrots
- 4 celery stalks
- 1/2 t. salt
- 1/2 t. pepper

In a large covered pot, put all the ingredients. Bring to a boil.

Set to a medium temperature and let cook for 1 and 1/2 hours.

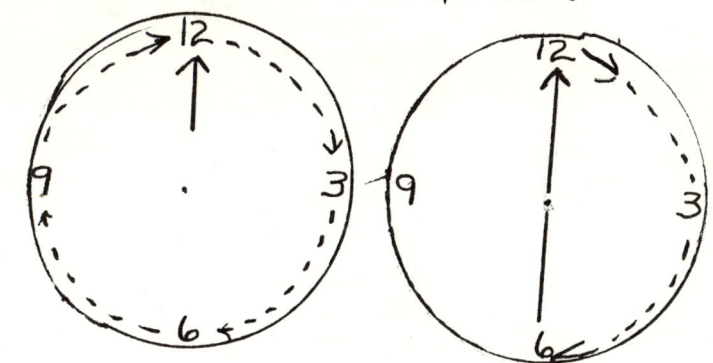

Serve hot with noodles.

CHICKEN

You will need:

    5 lb. chicken, cleaned and washed   2 t. garlic salt
    3 T. margarine   2 t. paprika

In a dish, mix together the salt, paprika and margarine. Rub over the chicken.

Put in a large baking pan. Cover loosely with foil.

Set the oven to 350°.

Bake in the oven for 2 1/2 hours.

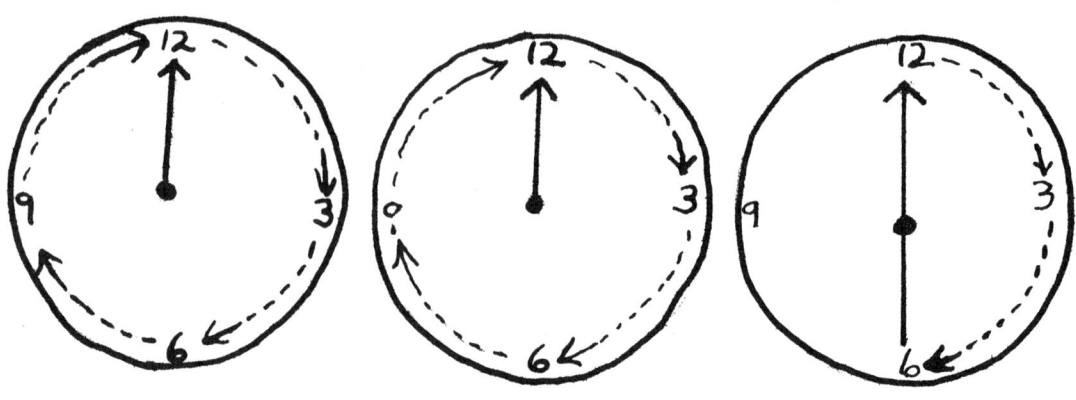

CARROT PUDDING

You will need:

    2 lb. cans of sliced carrots   4 T. sugar
    4 eggs   1 t. baking powder
    4 T. flour   1 t. vanilla
    4 T. margarine

In a bowl, mash together the carrots, eggs, flour, margarine, sugar, baking powder, and the vanilla.

Pour into an 8 inch square pan.

Set the oven to 350°.

Bake in the oven for 35 minutes.

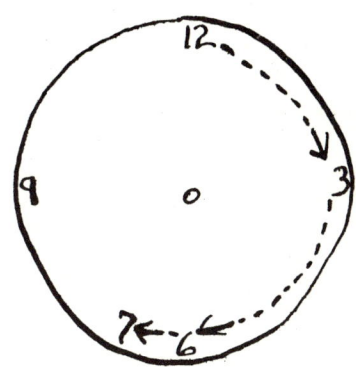

STRUDEL

You will need:

    2 c. flour
    1/4 t. salt
    1 egg white
    1 c. chopped walnuts (optional)

    2/3 c. warm water
    1/3 c. oil
    apricot jam

In a bowl mix flour, salt, water, oil and egg white to make dough.

Divide dough into 4 pieces and roll each piece flat with a rolling pin.

Fill with jam and nuts (if desired). Roll up like a jelly roll and place on lightly greased cookie sheet.

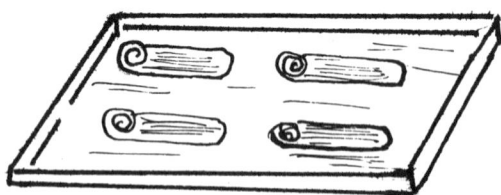

Set oven to 350°.

Bake in the oven for 35 minutes or until golden brown. Cool and slice.

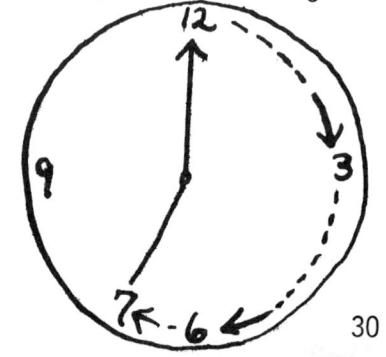

30

Pre-School Up

YOM TOV FRUIT OR NUT BOWL

Young children will need supervision with this paper-maché project.

You will need:

    plastic bowl (cereal size is good)　　　bowl of water
    paste　　　　　　　　　　　　　　　　　　paint or felt tip pens
    water　　　　　　　　　　　　　　　　　　any kind of grease, oil,
    cup　　　　　　　　　　　　　　　　　　　　　vaseline
    old newspapers　　　　　　　　　　　　large paint brush for paste

---

1. Grease the bowl all over lightly.

2. Make a small amount of paste in the cup and leave for the time it tells you on paste container.

---

3. Tear up a newspaper in small pieces. Let the pieces soak in bowl of water for a minute, then take them out.

4. With the empty bowl upside down, paste the newspaper, a piece at a time, to the bowl. You can use the brush to put on the paste. Use plenty of paste.

---

5. Make sure the bowl is completely covered. Then paste on several more overlapping layers.

6. Leave to dry in a warm place for a day or two. (May be speeded up by using a _warm_ oven.) When dry, remove the plastic bowl.

---

7. After the bowl is dry, you may paint or color it. To waterproof it, use a coat of clear shellac after paint is dry.

32

Pre-School
Up

NEW YEAR GREETING CARD HOLDER

You will need:

    oatmeal box
    yarn
    paint
    scissors

---

1. Remove both ends from oatmeal box.

2. Paint box.

---

3. Wind yarn around and around from inside to outside until box is uniformly but not totally covered and then knot on inside to secure.

4. Cards are inserted behind one strand of yarn. Yarn in middle of opened card will hold it in place.

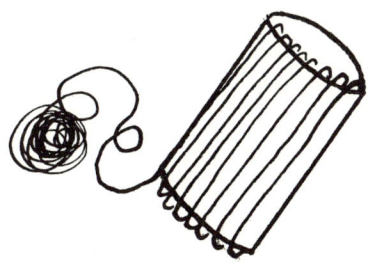

---

5. Present to Mother and Dad for a Happy New Year surprise!

33

PUZZLE NEW YEAR CARDS

You will need:

    piece of cardboard (not too thick)
    pencil
    paint, felt tip pens, or crayons
    scissors
    large envelope

---

1. Draw a New Year design on the cardboard with a pencil.

2. Color in the picture. Fill in the whole area of the cardboard except your name.

---

3. Draw lines across the cardboard in different shapes.

4. Cut along the lines carefully. Then put the pieces into an envelope and mail.

Pre-School
Up

SPATTER NEW YEAR CARDS

You will need:

    paper cut to fit envelope size   small container of water
    envelopes   small piece of cardboard
    old toothbrush   framed piece of screening
    poster paint   scissors

---

1. Cut out Jewish holiday symbol from cardboard.

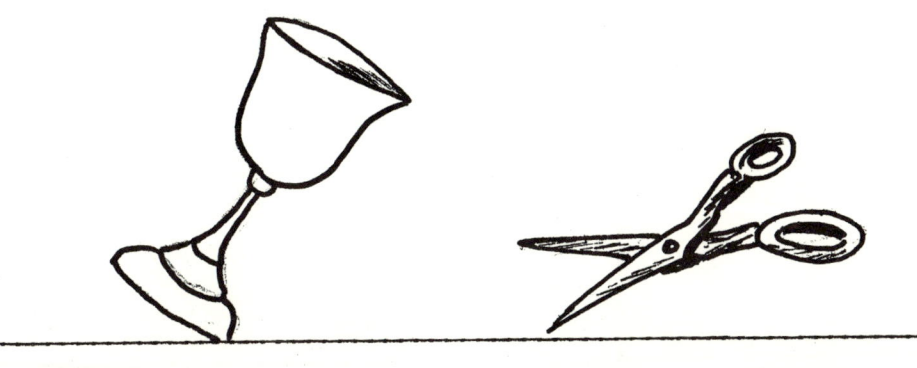

2. Place cardboard figure on paper. Place framed screen on top. Dip toothbrush in diluted mixture of paint and water and scrub across screen. Continue until spattering of paint covers paper.

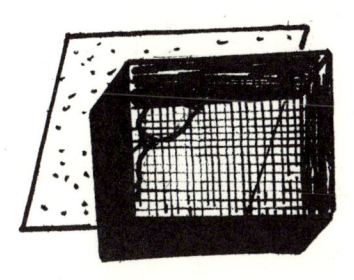

---

3. When dry, write your New Year greeting inside or on back of card, put in envelope, and mail!

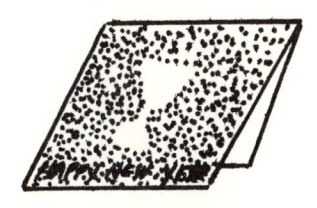

NEW YEAR MOSAIC

You will need:

    small stones or aquarium chips
    white glue
    yarn
    thick cardboard

---

1. Glue border around cardboard and press yarn on going around and around frame to make border.

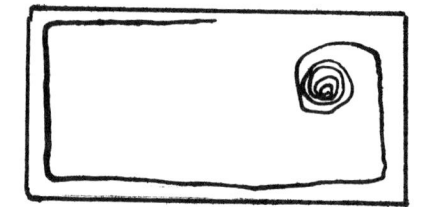

2. Draw a simple holiday figure with glue.

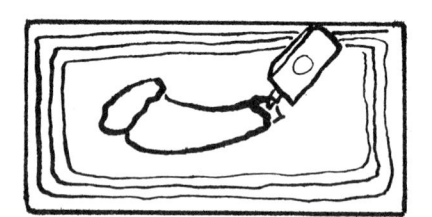

3. Press yarn onto outline drawing of glue.

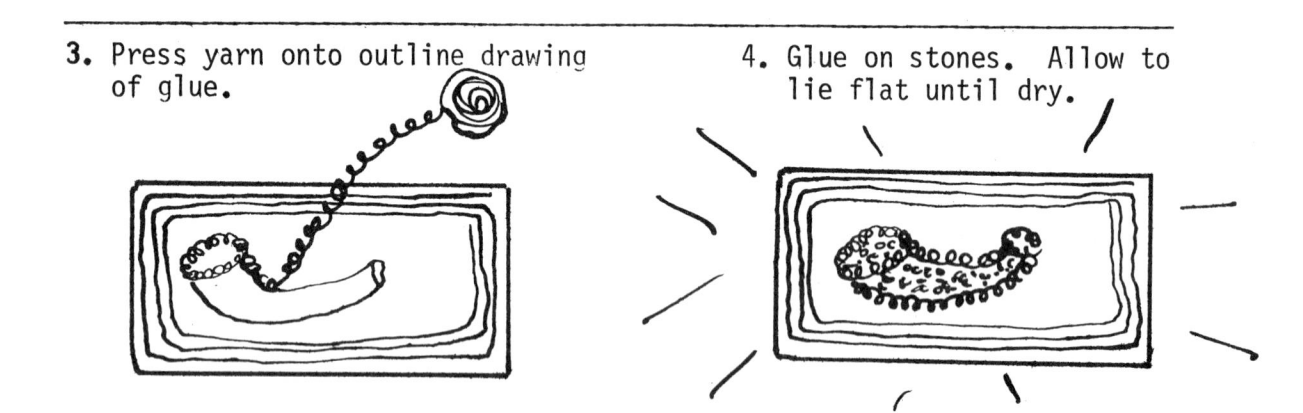

4. Glue on stones. Allow to lie flat until dry.

Pre-School
Up

NEW YEAR MOSAIC

You will need:

    white paper   crayon
    scraps of colored paper   scissors
    white glue

---

1. With your crayon, draw a simple holiday symbol.

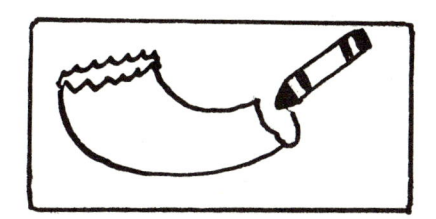

2. Cut colored scrap paper into tiny bits of paper.

---

3. Spread glue inside the crayoned holiday symbol.

4. Sprinkle the bits of colored paper on the glued part, wait a minute, then shake off extra bits.

Pre-School
Up

MAGEN DAVID
(Star of David)

You will need:

    6 popsicle sticks   sparkles
    paste   pieces of string
    acrylics

---

1. Paste 3 popsicle sticks into a triangle.

2. Paste the other 3 popsicle sticks into a triangle.

3. When both triangles are dry, place one over the other in the shape of a star and paste them together.

4. Decorate your star on both sides any way you would like.

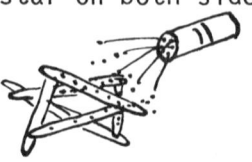

5. Fasten one end of the string to your Magen David and hang it up!

HAPPY NEW YEAR!

Traditional Hasidic Tune
Words by Gail Kansky

Hap-py New Year! Hap-py New Year! We will pray for God's for-give-ness -.
We will pray for love and kind-ness -.

Show re-pen-tence, Show our care, Raise our voice so loud in prayer. Hear us, Oh Lord, we now be-seech thee! -seech thee!

© Gail Kansky 1976

L'SHANA TOVA

Words and Music by Judy Sacks

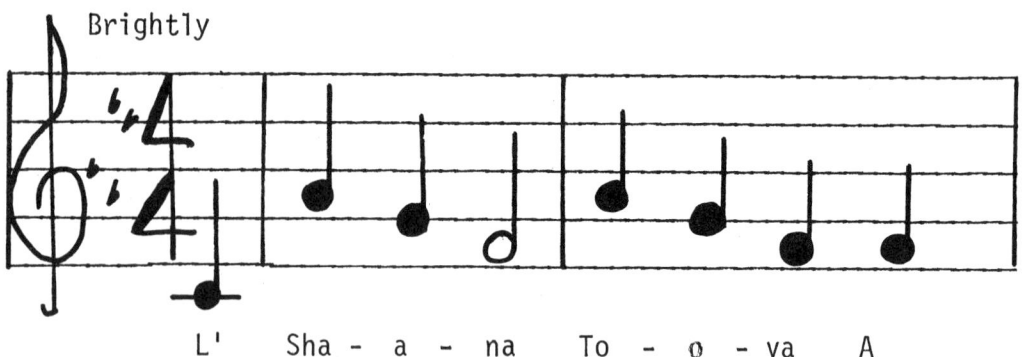

Brightly

L' Sha - a - na To - o - va A
We wish you health hap - pi - ness and

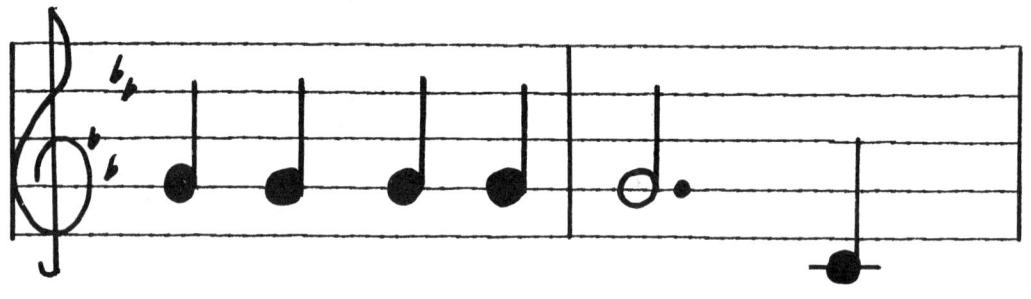

sweet and hap - py year. L'
love the whole year through. L'

sha - a - na To - o - va to
sha - a - na To - o - va, a

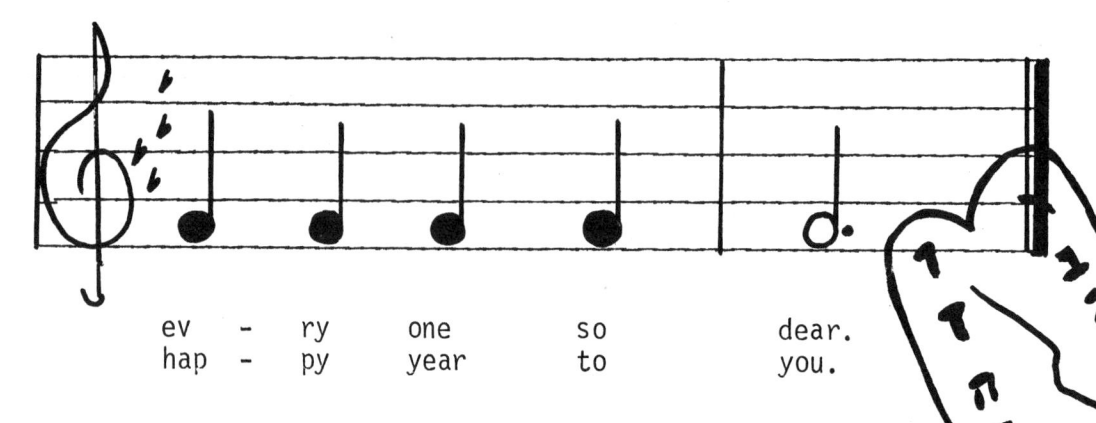

ev - 'ry one so dear.
hap - py year to you.

© Judy Sacks 1976

ROSH HASHANAH!

Music by Jay Englander
Words by Gail Kansky

Rosh Ha-sha-nah! Rosh Ha-sha-nah! The be-gin-ning of the new year.

Rosh Ha-sha-nah! Rosh Ha-sha-nah! Sho-far sounds call out clear.

For-give us for our sins. Bring good health to our kith and kin.

Bring us peace near and far. We wish all L'Sha- Na To - va!

@ Gail Kansky, Jay Englander 1976

DANCE TO "ROSH HASHANAH!"

1. Join hands in a circle.

2. First two measures of song:

    a. Right foot cross in front of left foot. Bring right foot back beside left.

    b. Left foot cross in front of right foot. Bring left foot back beside right.

3. Measures 3 and 4:

    a. Right foot steps sideways.

    b. Left brought up beside right.

    c. Repeat 3 more times (total of four side-steps).

4. Repeat 2 and 3 (next 4 measures).

5. Measures 9, 10:

    a. Circle moves toward center (5 steps) raising hands (still joined) upward toward center.

6. Measures 11, 12:

    a. Circle steps backward to original position (5 steps), dropping hands to normal position.

7. Measures 13-16:

    Repeat 5, 6.

ADDITIONAL SONGS FOR ROSH HASHANAH

TITLE	SOURCE
"L'shana Tova"	SWS, MSWS
"Sh'ma Yisrael"	SWS
"Zohrenu"	SWS
"Jubilant Song"	MMYO
"Toembai"	MMYO
"V'hol Ma'aminim"	MSWS

JEWISH SYMBOL "CONCENTRATION"

You will need:

   large piece of cardboard (giftboxes make good cardboard)
   pens, crayons, or markers
   ruler
   scissors

Cut the cardboard into 16 squares. Make the squares all the same size so that they all look alike. On one side of the square draw a Jewish symbol. Make two cards with that symbol. There are many to choose from such as Shabbat candles, star, Torah, wine cup. You should have 8 different symbols in all. Turn the squares over and mix them all up. Arrange them on a table and play "concentration." Each player turns over 2 squares trying to match them. (A match is two squares with the same symbol.) Whoever gets a match keeps the squares. Whoever makes the most matches...wins!

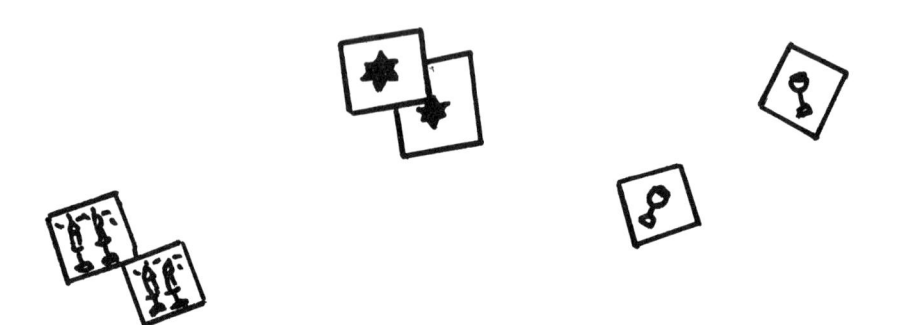

44

BEANBAG PLAYMATES

You will need:

    beanbags (empty)   dreidle
    mezzuzeh   candle
    star   kiddush cup
    prayer book   other holiday items

Fill beanbags with holiday objects. Let the children feel each beanbag and guess what item is in the bag. Every time he guesses correctly, he receives a point. Who can get the most points?

WHERE DO I BELONG?

You will need:

    pencil
    paper

Children sit in a circle. The child in the center of the circle writes the name of a Judaic object on a piece of paper. The other children must guess what word he has written by asking him questions. The child who guesses the correct word takes his place in the center.

    Example:
    Questions   Does it go on the wall?   yes
                         Does it go in a bookcase? no
                         Do you wear it?   no
                         Do you play with it?   no
    Answer   Mezzuzeh

TRAVELLING THROUGH ISRAEL

You will need:

    map of Israel
    ball

Children stand in a circle. A player stands in the center, throws the ball into the air and calls the name of a city or town in Israel. The child who can locate the place on the map runs forward and catches the ball. He goes over to the map and points to it.

> Example: Throw the ball in the air and call "Natanya." The child to catch the ball gets to point to it on the map.

LIGHT THE CANDLES

You will need:

    blackboard
    chalk

Children form 2 lines facing the blackboard. The first child in each line goes up to the blackboard and draws a menorah. The second child in each line draws the Shamos. The next child in the line draws the first candle in the menorah. Each succeeding child draws a candle until all 8 candles are in place. The next child draws a flame on the first candle. Each child in line adds a flame to the other candles until all the candles are "LIT." The team to finish first, wins.

A SIMPLE ROAST

You will need:

    4 lb. shoulder roast   1 package of onion soup mix
    aluminum foil   fork

In a roasting pan place a large piece of foil. Empty half the package of onion soup mix onto it.

Put the roast in the pan, pour over the remaining package of soup mix.

Pinch the foil together to cover the roast. Poke holes in the top of the foil with a fork.

Set the oven to 350°.

Bake in the oven for 2 hours or more. (This depends on whether you like your meat rare, medium, or well-done.)

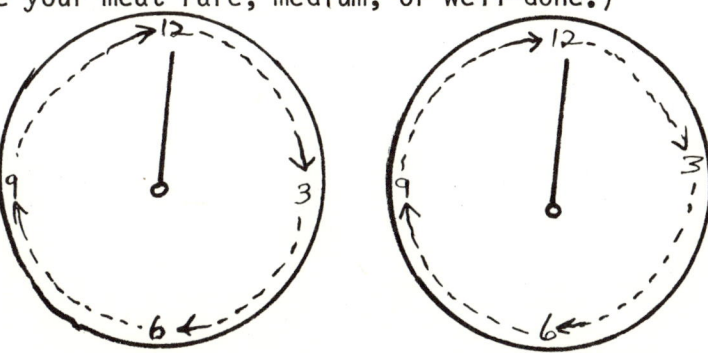

STRINGBEANS FONTAINEBLEAU

You will need:

    2 T. instant onions
    1 can sliced mushrooms
    2 T. butter or margarine
    1 tall can French style stringbeans

In a bowl, mix all the ingredients.

Lightly grease an 8" square pan. Pour the mixture into the pan.

Set the oven to 350°.

Bake in the oven for 20 minutes.

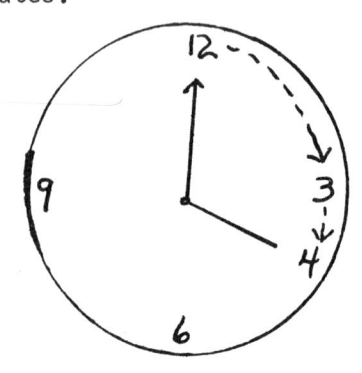

CARROT TZIMMES

You will need:

    1 large can sliced carrots   3 T. butter or margarine
    1 can sweet potatoes (sliced)   1 c. water
        or   1/2 c. honey
    1 can yams (sliced)   1/2 c. brown sugar
    1 can apple filling   1 t. cinnamon
    1 t. salt

In a 2 quart baking dish, place a layer of carrots, a layer of potatoes, then a layer of apples.

Repeat, adding another layer of carrots, potatoes, and apples.

In a bowl, mix water, honey, sugar, cinnamon, salt, and margarine together.

Pour the mixture over the layers in the baking dish.

Set the oven to 350°.

Bake in the oven for 35 minutes.

SPONGE CAKE

You will need:

   6 eggs   1/4 c. lemon juice
   1 c. sugar   1/4 c. orange juice
   1 c. flour   1 t. baking powder

Separate egg whites from yolks into a bowl.

In another bowl beat egg yolks, sugar, flour, baking powder, orange juice and lemon juice together to make batter.

Beat egg whites with a pinch of salt until stiff. Fold into batter.

Pour batter mixture into ungreased 10" tube pan.

Set the oven to 325°.

Bake in the oven for 1 hour.

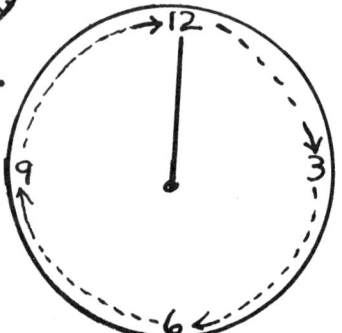

NO BAKE COOKIES

You will need:

   2.c. sugar
   1/2 c. milk
   1/4 lb. margarine
   2 T. cocoa

   1/2 c. peanut butter
   vanilla (to taste)
   3 c. quick rolled oats
       (more if needed to thicken)

In a pot combine the sugar, milk, margarine, and cocoa. <u>Boil</u> these together for 1 minute.

Add the other ingredients.

Drop batter one teaspoon at a time onto waxed paper and cool for 1/2 hour in the refrigerator.

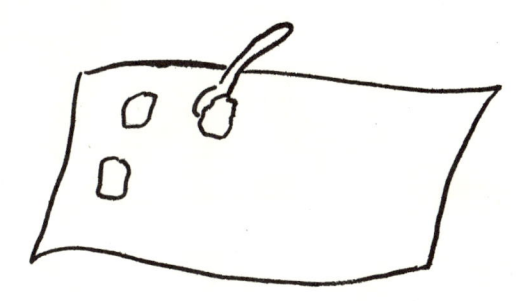

Succot and Simchat Torah

Pre-School Up

SUCCAH DECORATIONS

You will need:

    straws   glue
    peanuts   glitter
    paint   needle
                              scissors

1. Paint peanuts. Glue glitter to some straws or nuts.

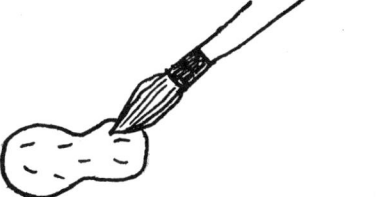

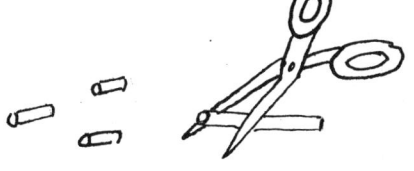

2. Cut straws into about 1" pieces.

3. Thread needle and string together separate chains of peanuts and straws or string them together.

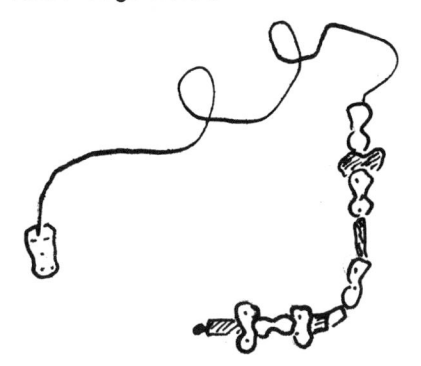

4. Hang on succah walls. You can also try stringing cranberries and popcorn for decorations.

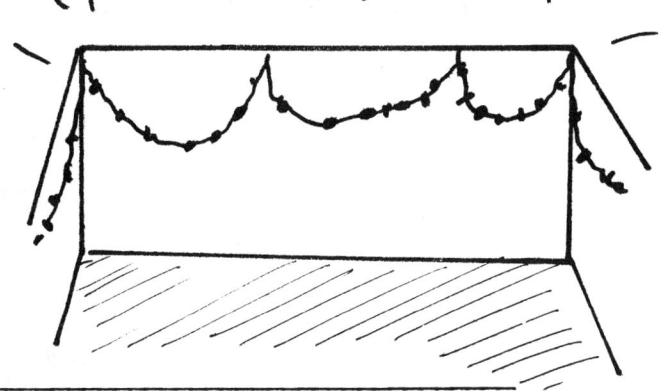

STAR OF DAVID

You will need:

   paper
   scissors

---

1. Start with a circle. If you don't have a perfect circle, then follow these directions:

   a. Fold a square piece of paper in half. Then fold it in half again.

   b. Make a curved cut as shown below on the part of the square that has no folded edges.

---

2. Now fold your circle in half (a), then in thirds (b), then in half again (c).

   a.   b.   c.

---

3. The folds last pressed down must be cut off. When opened, you have a pattern for the Star of David that may be used for decorations or any project you wish. For a larger star, start with a large circle; for a smaller one, start with a smaller circle.

---

4. To make your star three-dimensional, cut three of different colors, pin them (common pin) together in the middle, then bend out sides.

PRETZELS

(to hang up as Succah decorations)

You will need:

- 1 packet of yeast
- 4 c. flour
- 1 1/2 c. warm water

- 1 T. sugar
- 1 t. salt
- 1 egg
- kosher (coarse) salt

In a bowl mix the yeast into 1 1/2 cups warm water.

Add sugar and salt.

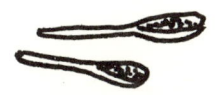

Stir in the 4 cups of flour.

Place the dough on the table and knead it until it is smooth.

Cut off small pieces and roll them with your hands to make "ropes."

PRETZELS (continued)

Shape the ropes into pretzels.

Put the pretzels on a cookie sheet and brush with beaten egg. Then sprinkle kosher (coarse) salt over them.

Set oven to 450°.

Bake for 12-15 minutes or until golden brown.

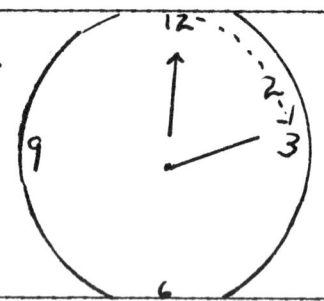

When your pretzels have cooled hang them with string in your Succah!

CARROT PLANT

You will need:

    carrot
    knife
    string
    water

---

1. Have someone help scoop out the inside of the carrot after cutting away the pointed end. Scoop out about two inches.

2. Punch a hole on each side of the scooped out part and attach a string to hang your carrot.

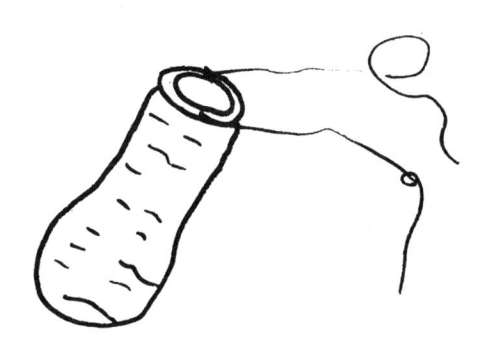

---

3. Hang your carrot in a window and fill the vase part with water. Keep the carrot filled with water and the bottom will soon have a pretty fern-like growth. When your Succah is built, hang your carrot vase there for a decoration.

BRIGHT CENTERPIECE FRUITS

You will need:

    clay   pencil
    water   liquid wax
    paint   knife

---

1. Shape the main part of each piece of fruit you are making. (Start with a ball for an orange or apple, press in a hollow for the top.) Use the pencil to mark the clay. (For example, criss-cross a pineapple with the point, press a small hole in the center of each criss-cross.

---

2. Out of a flattened piece of clay, cut out two leaves (or more, depending on fruit). Cut out stems. Wet the end of the stem and press it onto fruit. Wet the ends of the leaves and press them onto the stem.

---

3. When your clay is dry, paint with appropriate colors.

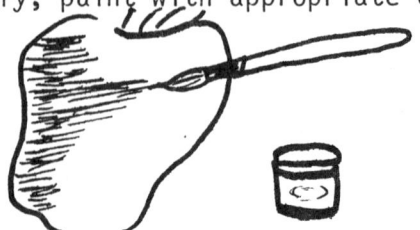

---

4. When the paint is dry, pour liquid wax over fruit. (Be sure to protect your working surface with newspaper.) Let dry, then arrange fruit in a basket or bowl for your holiday centerpiece.

HOLY ARK MODEL

You will need:

    cereal box (small) or other similar box
    paste
    construction paper (or foil)
    bottle cap
    birthday candle

1. Perforate front opening of cereal box. If other box is used, cut in same way.

2. Paste paper to cover box (or paint if easier). Foil can be used as well.

3. Paste a star above opening.

4. Glue bottle cap to top for eternal light and secure candle.

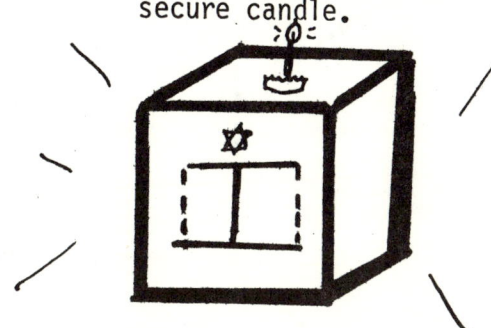

Pre-School
Up

SIMCHAT TORAH FLAG

You will need:

    paper
    crayons or paint
    paste, tape, or stapler

---

1. Cut a piece of paper as shown below and decorate with paint or crayons.

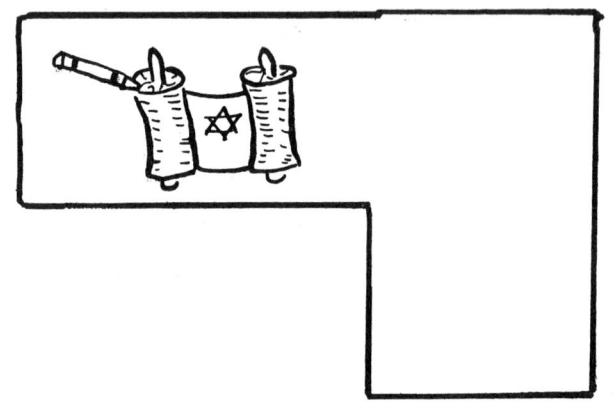

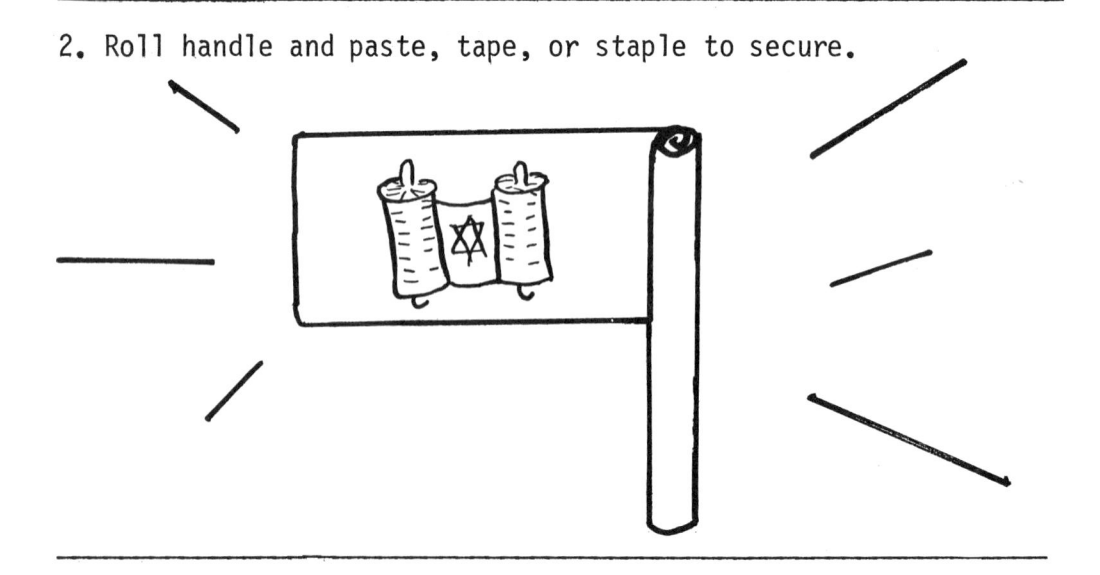

---

2. Roll handle and paste, tape, or staple to secure.

Pre-School Up

YARN AND PIN PICTURE

You will need:

    flat piece of styrofoam
    push-pins with knob heads
    yarn

---

1. Push the pins 3/4 of the way into the styrofoam. Older children can push them in to form an outline of an appropriate holiday symbol.

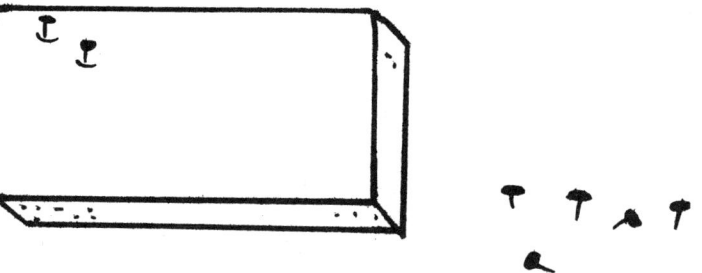

---

2. Wind yarn around pins to form a pretty design.

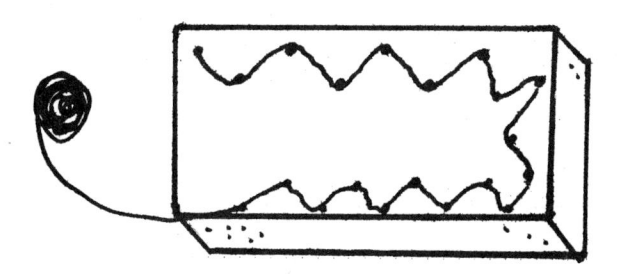

---

3. Push pins firmly down to help hold picture in place.

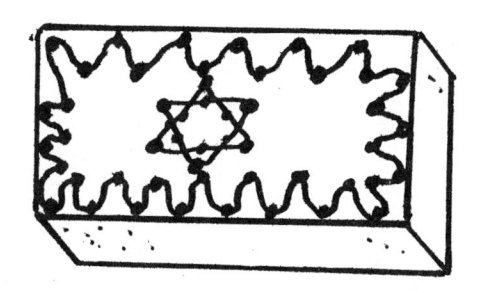

SUCCOT SONG

Music by Jay Englander
Words by Gail Kansky

Brightly and crisply

See the ap - ples red and ro - sy?
Hold your juice to say the bles - sing,
(wine)

See the grapes so plump and green?
"Thank you God, for ev - ry thing."

Hang them high in the Su - cah. Is-nt it
Af - ter we all eat our meal. Joy-ful- ly

the grand - est you've ev - er seen?
we'll raise our voice and we'll sing.

© Gail Kansky, Jay Englander 1976

THE SUCCAH

Music by Jay Englander
Words by Gail Kansky

Lightly

Bang! Goes the ham-mer, the Suc-cah's built high.

Bran-ches on top to look up at the sky!

Night-time comes ear-ly and when I look up,

Blue skies are gone And it's stars that I spy!

© Gail Kansky, Jay Englander 1976

ZUM GALI, GALI

Adapted and edited with new words
by Gail Kansky
(based on traditional Israeli song)

Moderately

Zum ga-li, ga-li, ga-li. Zum ga-li, ga-li.

Chorus: zum ga-li ga-li ga-li zum ga-li ga-li
Solo: As we work we'll sing loud and clear
        He-cha lutz le'-man a-vo-dah.

Work was made for the pi-o-neer.
A-vo-dah le'-man he-cha-lutz.

Zum ga-li ga-li ga-li. Zum ga-li ga-li. Zum-m Zum-m ZUM!
(shout)

© Gail Kansky 1976

ADDITIONAL SONGS FOR SUKKOT AND SIMHAT TORAH

TITLE	SOURCES
"Open the Gates"	SWS
"Lama Sukkah Zu"	SWS, NJSB, MSWS
"Sisu V'simhu"	SWS, NJSB, MSWS
"Yom Tov Lanu"	SWS, NJSB
"Harvest Song"	SWS, TIM, NJSB, MSWS
"Ono Adonoi"	SWS
"Kaha N'rakeda"	SWS
"Ki V'simha"	SWS, MSWS
"Mazurka"	MM
"Song of the Lulav"	MSWS
"Simhat Torah"	MSWS

THINGS ALONG THE WAY

Children sit in a circle. Each child is named an object he might see when he takes a trip. A player sits in the center of the circle and the leader or teacher reads a story with the object words. Whenever an object is read that has the same name as a child in the circle, that child must run around the circle and return to his place before the child in the center can tag him and take his place.

MIXUP

The child who is "it" says a sentence that is either mixed up or backwards. Another child must repeat the sentence in the correct order.

> Example: "Walls tumbling and the battle came fought down the Jericho.
>
> Answer: "Joshua fought the battle of Jericho
> And the walls came tumbling down."

THE ETROG

Children sit in a circle with their hands behind their backs. One child sits in the center of the circle and closes his eyes. The children sing a Hebrew song. The teacher places a button in the hands of one of the children. As the children sing, the children pass the button behind them. At any time during the singing, the child in the center may say "stop". Everything must stop, the singing and the passing of the botton, or etrog. The child in the center must guess who has the button or etrog. If the guess is correct, he changes places with that child and the game continues.

SCRAMBLED EGGS

You will need:

    blackboard   chalk
    paper   pencils

The following words are put on the board. The children must unscramble the words to find the holidays and holiday symbols. A point is given for each correct word.

EXAMPLE	ANSWER
hhanaucka	Chanukah
llahcha	challah
ezzhumeh	mezzuzeh
elancd	candle
lliatt	tallit
ursed	sedur
zotam	matzo
uthr	Ruth
hhanna	Hannah
horta	Torah

CATCH ME IF YOU CAN.

The children stand in a circle. The leader names a holiday and follows it with words that are related to that holiday. If the word given is correct, the children clap; if the word given is incorrect, they must sit down. The first child to sit down and catch the wrong word gets to be the leader.

EXAMPLE	ANSWER
Chanukah	
candle	clap
macabees	clap
rain	the first child to sit down takes the leader's place

SWEET POTATO DELIGHT

You will need:

    1 lb. can of sweet potatoes, drained
    1 small can of crushed pineapple
    Marshmallow Fluff

In a bowl, mix together the sweet potatoes and the crushed pineapple.

Pour into an 8 inch square baking dish. Cover the mixture with Marshmallow Fluff.

Set the oven to 350°.

Bake in the oven for 30 minutes.

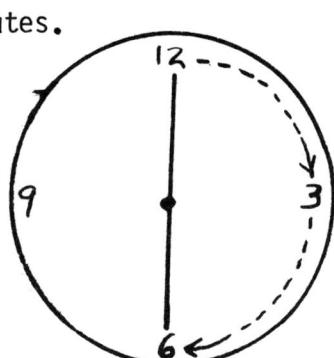

SALMON LOAF

You will need:

    1 large can of pink salmon   1 T. minced onions
    3 eggs   1/2 t. salt
    3/4 c. milk   1/2 t. pepper
    1/2 c. corn flake crumbs   1 small can mushrooms

In a large bowl, combine all the above ingredients. Mix well.

Pour into a well greased 9" x 13" pan.

Set the oven to 325°.

Bake in the oven for 1 hour.

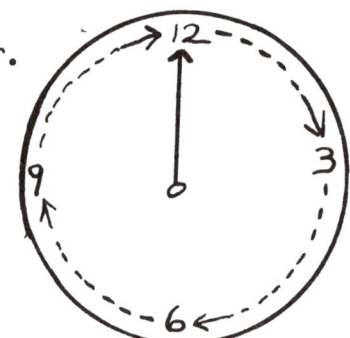

MUNDEL BREAD

You will need:

   3 eggs
   1 c. sugar
   1 t. vanilla
   1/2 c. salad oil
   3 c. flour

   1 c. chopped walnuts
      (optional)
   1/2 t. salt
   1 jar dried cherries
   2 t. baking powder

In a bowl, beat egss, sugar, vanilla, and oil together.

Add flour, salt, and baking powder. Mix well. Add dried cherries and walnuts (if desired).

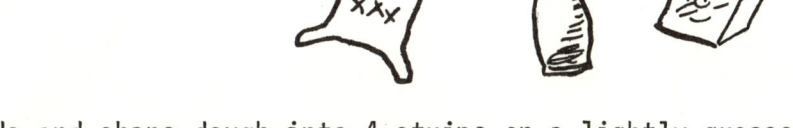

Wet hands and shape dough into 4 strips on a lightly greased cookie sheet.

Set oven to 375°.

Bake in the oven for 25 minutes or until golden brown.

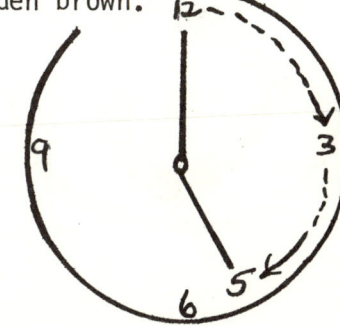

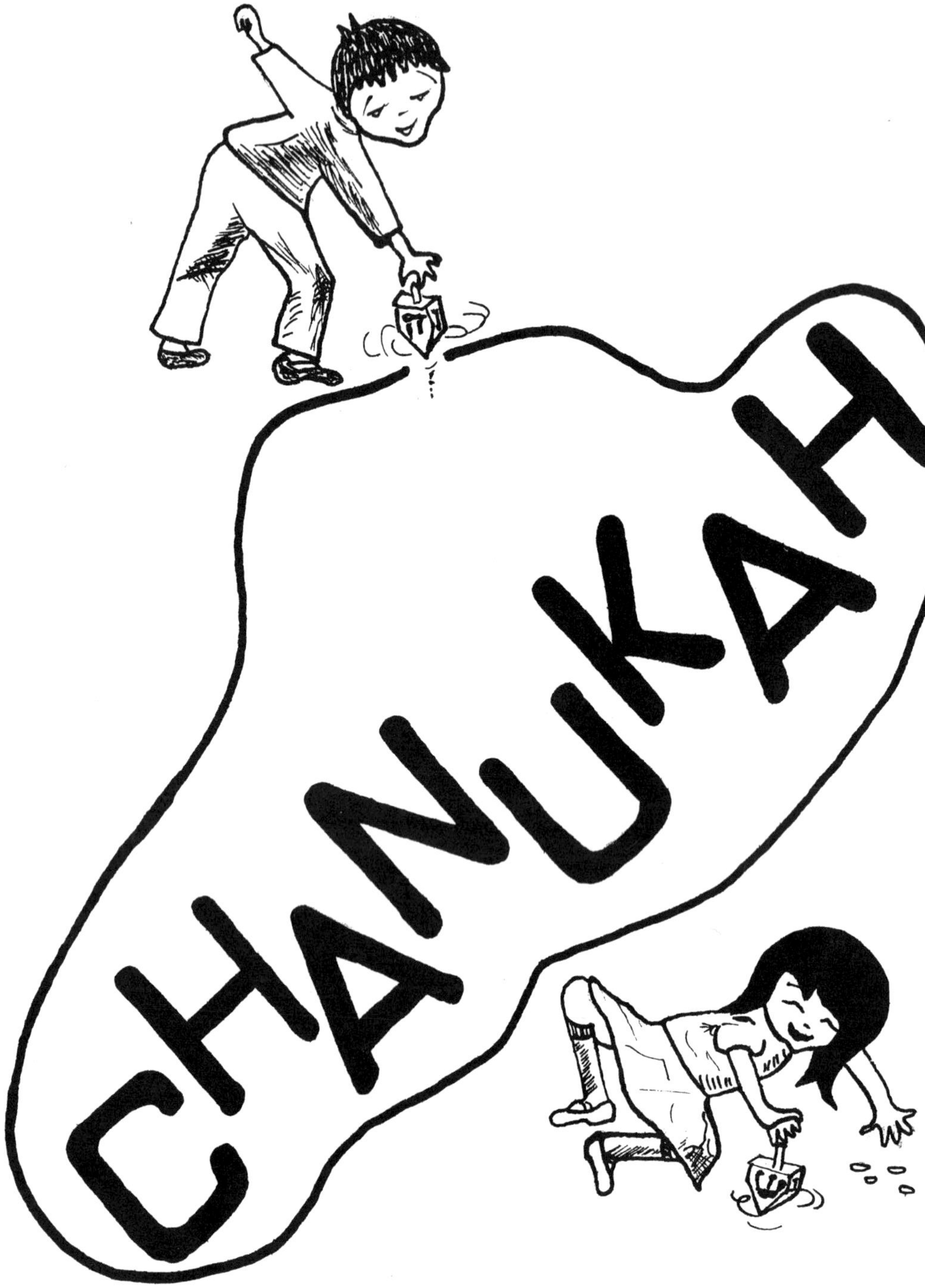
CHANUKAH

CLAY DREIDLE

You will need:

    jack   brushes
    self-hardening clay or plaster   paper cup
         of paris   lacquer
    sandpaper
    paints

---

1. Mix plaster of paris in cup to consistency of cream. Mold dreidle.

2. Insert metal point on top of dreidle.

---

3. When completely dry, sand smooth with sandpaper.

4. Paint the letters hey, gimmel, shin, and nun, one for each side. Lacquer when dry.

Pre-School Up

MR. DREIDLE CENTERPIECE

You will need:

    construction paper   pencil
    crayons   scissors
    paste

---

1. Cut two identical Mr. Dreidles with extending arms and legs. (Draw one, cut out with blank paper underneath.)

---

2. Draw a face on each side of Mr. Dreidle. Cut slits in middle of bottom of one figure, and in middle of top in other.

---

3. Insert one Mr. Dreidle into slit of other. Your Mr. Dreidle is now free-standing!

Pre-School Up

EGG CARTON MENORAH

You will need:

   cardboard egg carton
   pipe cleaners
   paint
   clay or playing dough

---

1. Cut or tear off 3 sections of half the egg carton. Paint the carton.

---

2. Place pipe cleaners into each section with small amount of playing dough or clay to hold them upright.

---

3. What a nice present to give Mom and Dad for a centerpiece!

Pre-School
Up

DECORATIVE MENORAH

You will need:

    construction paper   crayons
    scissors   stapler
    paste

---

1. Fold paper in half. Unfold and decorate top half.

---

2. Fold bottom of paper in thirds folding down. Decorate bottom fold. Cut nine slits in middle fold. Staple corners of first third to top.

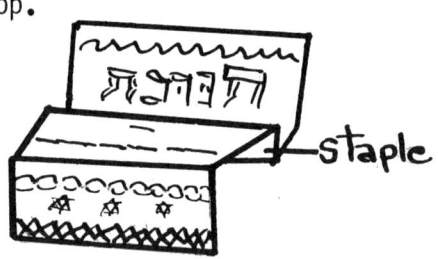

---

3. Cut and color candles and insert in slits. (The shamus and one more may be added each night for the eight nights.)

HOLIDAY GIFT WRAP

You will need:

   tissue paper
   small bowls of colored ink or
     food coloring in water
   pliers or snap clothespin
   newspapers or blotting paper
   warm iron

---

1. Fold the paper into a fan shape pleating it.

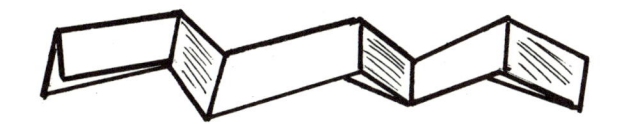

---

2. Next, fold the fan into triangles, squares, and rectangles.

---

3. Holding the paper with clothespin or pliers, dip one corner at a time into colored water. Hold it in water until the liquid draws up toward your clothespin. Then blot well.

---

4. Unfold carefully and let dry. Then press paper using a warm iron. You have changed plain tissue paper into dazzling gift wrap. Paste a piece of the extra wrap to paper for a matching card!

CHANUKAH MOBILE

To be a success, each figure should be the same weight as the others. If you find they are not, stick a tiny piece of paper to the lighter one to make it heavier, or cut a tiny bit off the heavier one.

You will need:

4 plastic straws	paints if plain paper used
adhesive tape	ruler
pencil	needle
plain or colored paper	thread
scissors	

---

1. Take two of the straws and tape lenghtwise, repeat for other two straws.

2. Place one double straw on top of other to make a cross. Tape around to secure.

3. Draw holiday figures at least 3" square. Then cut out. If coloring, do both sides.

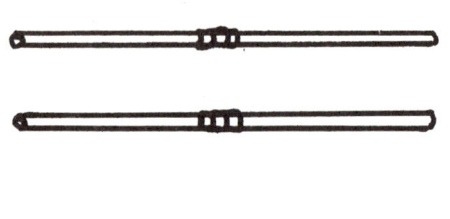

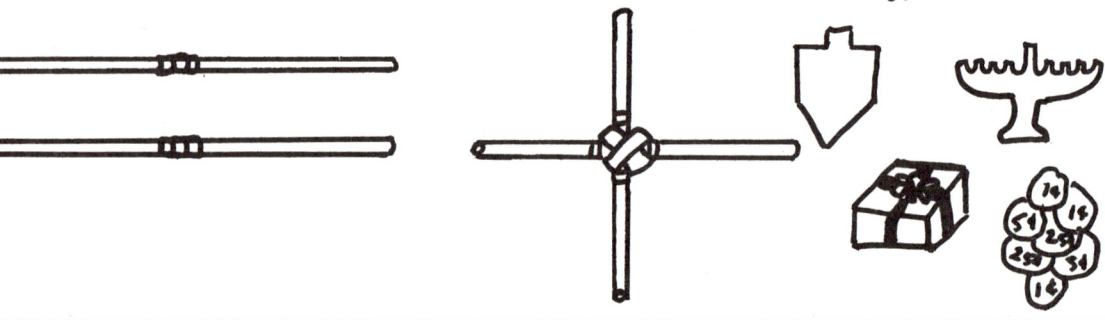

---

4. Cut a thread 24" long. Thread needle double and knot at end. Push through holiday figure.

5. Push needle through 1" from end of straw. Cut and knot thread. Repeat for other figures.

6. Thread needle again with double thread. Knot and push through middle of straws.

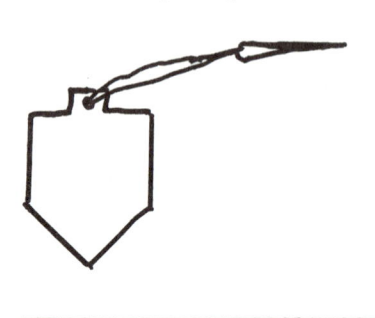

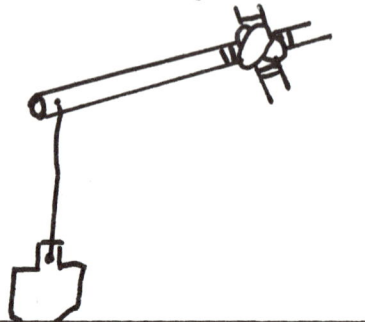

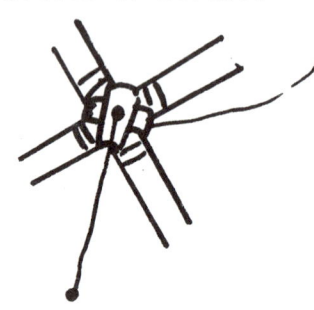

Now your mobile can be hung up.

78

DREIDLE PLACE CARD

You will need:

    long rectangular box (toothpaste
        box is good)
    pencil or dowel
    acrylic or poster paint
    glue (if using poster paint)

    paper
    pen
    tape
    ruler

---

1. Cut the box as shown below. Make the height before starting the point the same as the base measurement (dotted lines)

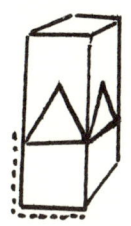

2. Tape the dreidle shut by bending the points together to form one point. Tape the lid closed, too.

---

3. Paint the box bottom and pencil or dowel. If using poster paint, mix with glue first.

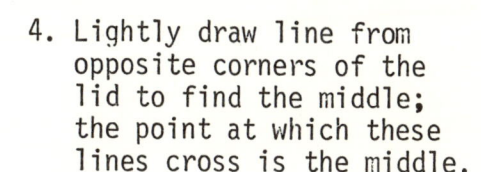

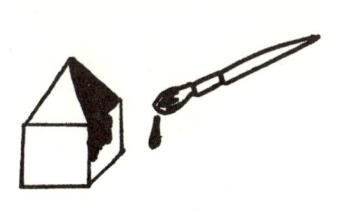

4. Lightly draw line from opposite corners of the lid to find the middle; the point at which these lines cross is the middle.

---

5. Insert the pencil or dowel into the center of the lid.

6. Attach a small piece of paper to the handle with tape and write the name on this paper. You may also paint letters on each side of the dreidle (Nun, Shin, Gimmel, Hey).

CHANUKAH DANCE

MUSIC: "MY DREYDLE" (see Additional Songs for Chanukah, page   )

Everyone join hands in a circle...Spread out so that your arms are nearly straight.

STEP I. Starting with <u>right</u> foot, take 4 steps into the center of the circle while at the same time raising your arms up high.

STEP II. Take 4 steps back starting again with right foot. Slowly lower your arms as you go back.

STEP III. Repeat Step I.

STEP IV. Repeat Step II.

STEP V. Starting on right foot and going to the right, take 8 sliding steps.

STEP VI. Repeat Step V to the LEFT.

This dance can be repeated many times with different variations. Steps I-IV should be repeated each time, and Steps V and VI (the chorus) can be changed each time. Below are some variations.

Variation #1: Hook right arms with your partner and swing around to the right for 8 counts. Repeat to the left hooking left arms.

Variation #2: Hold both hands of your partner and skip around to your right for 8 counts. Repeat to the left.

EIGHT CHANUKAH CANDLES

Music by Jay Englander
Words by Gail Kansky

Brightly

First light the Sha-mus and 1 can - dle's shi - ning.
First light the Sha-mus and 2 can - dle's shi - ning.
First light the Sha-mus and 3 can - dle's shi - ning.
First light the Sha-mus and 4 can - dle's shi - ning.
First light the Sha-mus and 5 can - dle's shi - ning.
First light the Sha-mus and 6 can - dle's shi - ning.
First light the Sha-mus and 7 can - dle's shi - ning.
First light the Sha-mus and 8 can - dle's shi - ning.

Lat - kes are fry - ing and We will all sing.
Pre - sents are o - pened and Drei-dles take wing.
Re - mind us of An - ti - o - cus the king.
Foes of the Ma - ca - bees feel-ing their sting.
Cel - e - brate joys that the mir - a - cles bring.
So few drops of oil that kept on burn - ing.
Flames that will help us in re - mem - ber - ing.
Tell us that we are re - ded - i - cat - ing.

@ Gail Kansky, Jay Englander 1976

DANCING 'ROUND THE MENORAH

Traditional Melody
Words by Gail Kansky

Gaily

First we light the can-dles. Then we will dance the ho - ra.
We re-call the miracle that set our peo-ple free. So

We will all join hands dan-cing round the Men - or- ah.
We will tell the sto- ry of Ju - dah Ma -ca- bee.

La la la la la la la la la La la la la la

la la la la la la la La la la la la la la la la la la la la

la la la la la la la la la la la la la la la la la la
la la la la la la la la la la la la la la la la la la la la
la la la la la la la la la la la
la la Chan - u - kah.

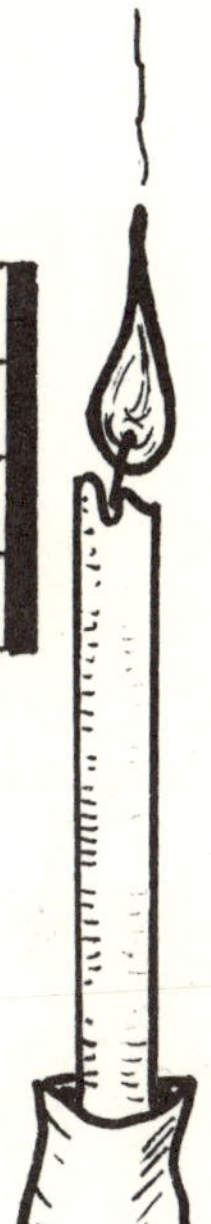

DANCE THE HORA!

TO "DANCING 'ROUND THE MENORAH"

The hora is a Palestinian pioneer dance.

1. Left foot steps to left.
2. Right foot behind left foot.
3. Jump with both feet together.
4. Kick with right foot, jump with both feet together.
5. Kick with left foot.
6. Repeat until end of music.

ADDITIONAL SONGS FOR CHANUKAH

TITLE	SOURCE
"Chanukah Blessing"	NJSB, CSP
"Mooz Tzur"	SWS, NJSB, MSWS, CSP
"My Candle"	SWS
"My Dreydle"	SWS, NJSB, MSWS
"Hanukah"	SWS, NJSB, MSWS
"Sivivon"	NJSB, MSWS
"Mi Y'mallel"	SWS, NJSB, MSWS, CSP
"The Chanukah Story"	CSP
"Candle Dance"	CSP
"When Chanukah Comes"	CSP
"Let's Make Latkes"	CSP
"Oy Chanukah"	CSP
"Sheleg Al H-aretz"	CSP
"Sing Along"	CSP
"Maccabee's March"	CSP
"Chanukah Rhythms"	CSP
"Mattathias Bold"	CSP
"Let's Play A Game of Dreydle"	CSP
"The Battle of Judah Macabee"	CSP
"A Chanukah Quiz"	CSP
"The Ballad of Emmaus"	CSP
"Sov, Sov, S'vivon"	SWS
"Y'Huda Hamakabi"	SWS
"Hear the Voice"	SWS

"Oh, Come My Dreydle"   SWS

"Al Hanisim"   SWS, NJSB, MSWS

"Hanukah Hymn"   MM

THE CHANUKAH GIFT BOX

Each child must name a Chanukah gift that starts with the initial of his first name. Go back and start again, naming a gift that starts with his last name. How many gifts can each child put into the box?

Example: David might say Dreidle

THE CANDLE AND THE MENORAH

Children stand in a circle. One player called "the candle" stands outside the circle. Another child called "the menorah" stands inside the circle. The child inside the circle must try to tag the child outside the circle. The children in the circle join hands and try to keep the menorah from tagging the candle.

A DOUGHNUT FOR TWO

(In Israel, doughnuts are a favorite Chanukah treat!)

You will need:

>a doughnut
>a long piece of string

Push a long string through the doughnut hole and tie a knot in the middle. Each of two players puts one end of the string into his or her mouth. When the signal is given, each player starts pulling as much string into his mouth, as quickly as possible. Players may use nothing but lips, tongue, and teeth. The player who reaches the doughnut first and bites off a piece - wins!

PANCAKES IN THE FRYING PAN

You will need:

>chalk
>straws (one per player)
>circles cut from construction paper

Draw a big circle on the floor with chalk. This is the "frying pan." At the other end of the room draw a line (the starting line). The players kneel behind the line, each holding a straw. In front of each player is a paper "pancake." Each player tries to move his pancake into the frying pan by blowing it with his straw. The player whose pancake reaches the frying pan first - wins!

SCRAMBLE

Each child is named a Hebrew letter. The child who is "it" closes his eyes and says, "scramble." The other children quickly change places. The child who is "it" must try to return the Hebrew letters to their original places. This game can be varied by giving the children names of holidays or Jewish heroes.

MACCABEES AND SYRIANS

Children stand in 2 lines about 3 feet apart facing each other. The team on one side of the line is called the Maccabees, the other team is called the Syrians. The player in the area between the 2 lines says "charge." The teams on either side of the line must try to get to the other team's side. The player in the middle must tag as many children from both teams as he can. These children must now stand with the caller and help him tag out the other children when he says "charge" again. The game continues until all the children have been tagged. The last child out becomes the new caller.

PINEAPPLE CHEESE NOODLE PUDDING
(KUGEL)

You will need:

- 8 oz. noodles
- 1 lb. cottage cheese
- 4 eggs
- 4 T. butter or margarine
- 2 t. vanilla
- 2 c. milk
- sugar
- 1 small can of crushed pineapple

In a large bowl, mix noodles, cottage cheese, eggs, margarine, vanilla, and pineapple.

Lightly grease a 9" x 13" pan.

Pour the mixture into a pan. Pour 2 cups of milk over the mixture.

Set the oven to 350°.

Bake in the oven for 1 hour.

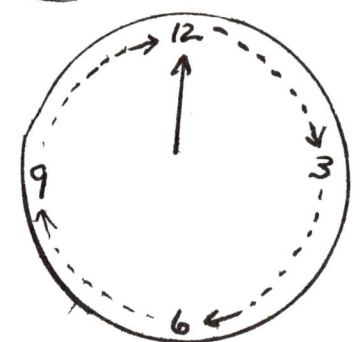

POTATO LATKES (PANCAKES)

You will need:

    1 package of instant potatoes   2 c. water
    2 T. butter or margarine   1 T. oil
    2 eggs   1 T. instant onions

In a pot on the stove, put in two cups of water, two tablespoons of butter or margarine, and bring to a boil.

Remove the pot from the stove and add one package of instant potatoes. Mix well.

Add two eggs and one tablespoon of instant onions. Mix well.

Place shallow pan on stove and melt oil. Turn to medium flame. Drop a tablespoon of batter into the pan for each pancake. When they are golden brown turn the pancakes over so that they cook on both sides.

Serve with sour cream or applesauce.

CHANUKAH PUNCH

You will need:

    2 trays of ice cubes
    2 bottles of ginger ale
    1/2 pint of orange sherbet

    1/2 c. sugar
    4 c. grape juice

In a large punch bowl, pour in all the ingredients. Add the sherbet. Let float.

Pour into individual cups. Most refreshing!

MOLDED SUGAR COOKIES

You will need:

    2 eggs
    4 c. flour
    1/2 t. salt
    2 t. baking powder

    1 c. oil
    2 T. lemon juice
    1 T. vanilla
    1 c. sugar

In a large bowl, mix all the ingredients together. The batter will be stiff.

With a rolling pin, roll the dough flat into a thin sheet.

Take a cookie cutter shaped like a star or a menorah and press down hard on the dough to cut out the shape.

Put on a lightly greased cookie sheet and sprinkle with cinammon and sugar.

Set the oven to 350°.

Bake in the oven for 20 minutes or until golden brown.

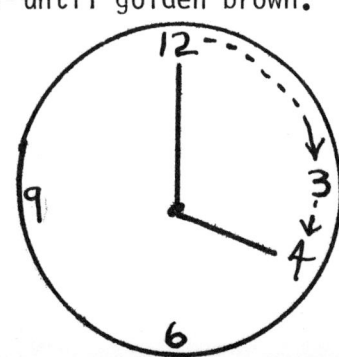

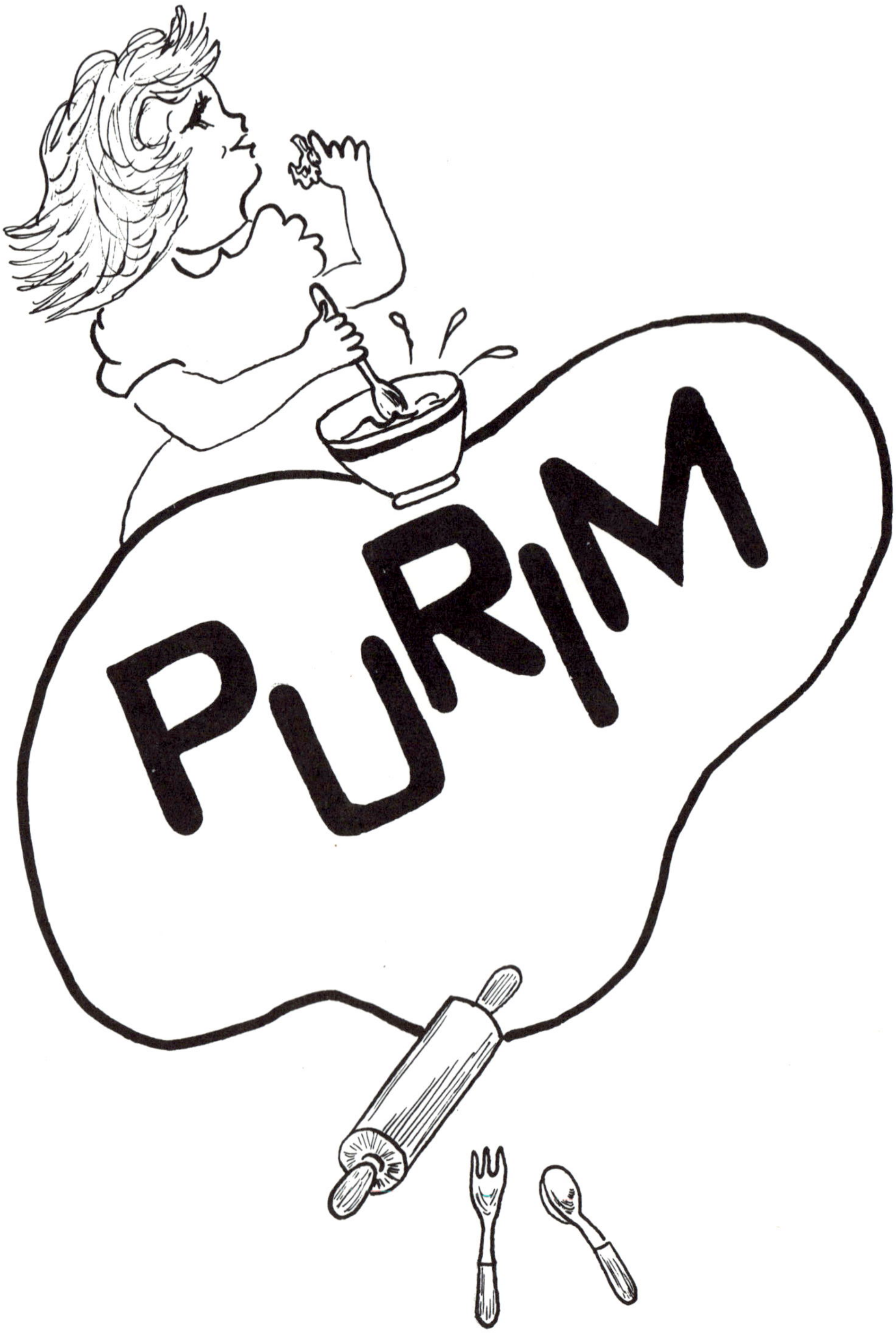
PURIM

Pre-School Up ✡

PURIM MASK

You will need:

    pieces of thin cardboard or
        9 inch paper plate
    pencil
    ruler
    scissors

    button or coin
    paints or felt tip pens
    hat elastic or string

---

1. Cut a circle out of cardboard or use a paper plate. Draw a line exactly across center of circle.

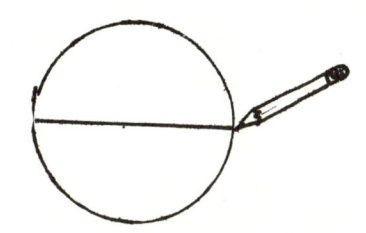

2. Mark the place for eyes by putting dots 2 3/4 inches apart and equally distant from the edge. Draw a circle around dots using coin or button. Cut out circles.

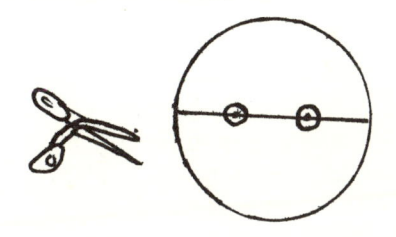

---

3. Draw a shape like you see below for the nose. Cut out sides and bottom to make a flap.

4. Tie string or elastic to holes about 1/2" from the edge near the eyes.

---

5. Try on your mask and mark where your mouth is. Then cut out a very small hole for mouth.

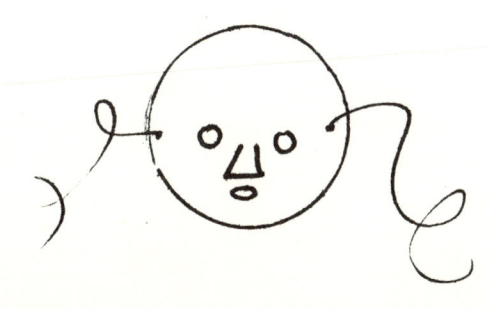

6. Paint or color your face the way you would like it. Use your own ideas. Wear with Purim costume.

NOAH'S ARK

You will need:

    large cereal box 7 1/2 x 11"
    another large box or cardboard
    4 1/2 x 10" cracker box
    construction paper
      (we used brown and orange)

    pipe cleaners
    glue
    scissors

---

1. The hull will be the cereal box. Cut some cardboard longer than the box to form the deck. Cut both ends to form points. Then paste the cardboard to the box.

2. Cover the deck with orange paper. Now cut out two pieces of brown paper 23" long and 3 1/2" wide for the sides. Glue them to the sides letting the top go higher to form a railing for the deck.

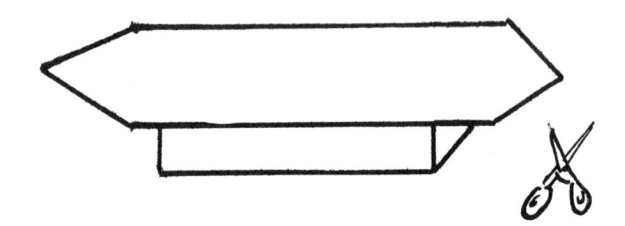

3. Cut the ends of the side paper curving up and ending in a point. Then glue the ends together.

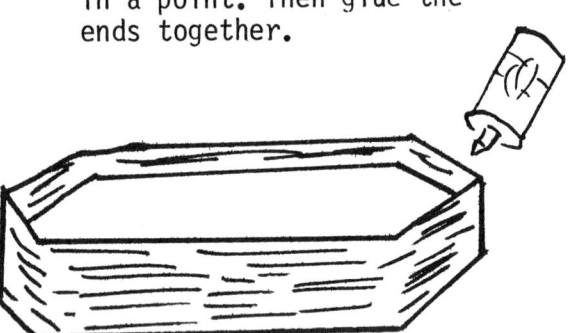

4. Cover the cracker box with orange paper for the house of the Ark. Before adding the door and windows of brown paper, cut the top of the house with pointed gables to set the roof upon.

5. The roof is made from brown paper cut to 8 x 11 1/2" long, folded in half the long way, and glued to the gables.

6. After gluing the house on the Ark, make a ladder from pipe cleaners. Cut two to about 5". Place them about an inch apart, and wind the rungs in place. Bend the top of the ladder into hooks and place it on the railing.

7. You may add your own animals to march by pairs into the Ark, or cut them out by folding paper and not cutting the fold when you cut out the animals. In this way, they will stand themselves.

Pre-School
Up

GIANT NOISEMAKER
(GREGGAR)

You will need:

    2 aluminum pie plates   white glue
    crepe paper streamer   scissors
    colored paper   pebbles, beans, or similar
    stapler

---

1. Place a few pebbles between two pie plates and staple the plates together.

2. Glue colored paper for design on noisemaker.

---

3. Staple on crepe paper streamers. Shake hard whenever Haman's name is mentioned.

Pre-School Up

BOX GREGGAR

You will need:

- box (matchbox or similar)
- lolipop stick or dowel
- aluminum foil
- tape
- paste or glue
- paper
- scissors
- rubber bands (2)
- seeds, pebbles, beans, or marbles

---

1. Place seeds or similar material in box. Tape box shut. Cover box with aluminum foil.

2. Pierce two holes in box and put stick or dowel through sides. Secure with rubber bands at top and bottom.

---

3. Glue colorful decorations to the foil.

PURIM WAX PRINT

You will need:

    candles or wax crayons
    small cooking pot or can
    knife
    box or small foil container
    paint

    turpentine
    ballpoint pen
    paper
    felt as big as box
    rag

---

1. Place your candles or crayons in a pot or can and put over low light on stove until melted.

2. Pour melted wax into box or foil container.

---

3. When wax is hard, remove it from container and smooth the surface of the wax with a knife. Then dip a rag into the turpentine and wipe the wax.

4. Use a ballpoint pen to scratch a design on the surface. Bear down hard to deepen the scratched lines. Make your design show a scene from the Purim story.

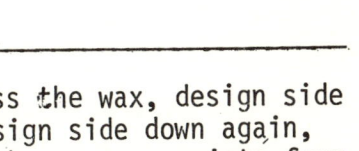

---

5. Now saturate the felt with poster paint, press the wax, design side down, onto the felt. Then press the wax, design side down again, onto your paper. Bear down hard. You can make as many prints from your wax as you wish!

Pre-School Up

QUEEN ESTHER'S CROWN

You will need:

    ruler   scissors
    pencil   aluminum foil
    colored paper   strong adhesive or stapler

1. Measure the colored paper 22" by 6" (or longer if your head is larger) and cut it out.

2. Cut large zig-zags along the edge.

3. Cut little circles or stars of foil and paste them onto paper.

4. Now stick (or staple) the ends of the paper together and let dry.

5. A straw with foil stars stapled at the end can be your sceptor!

7. One nine year old added long strips of slightly curled yellow paper to 3/4 of her crown so she could be a blond-haired Queen!

Pre-School Up

KING'S PURIM CROWN

You will need:

    two different colors of construction paper
    scissors
    glue
    stapler

---

1. Cut a strip of paper about 22 inches long and 2 inches wide.

---

2. Glue the strip into a headband to fit your head.

---

3. Now cut twenty 1" wide strips about 10 inches long.

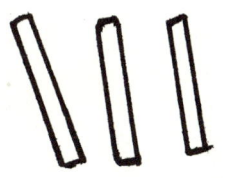

---

4. Staple the strips to the headband by putting the ends of the strip together without folding. Staple them to the inside, one next to the other, until the headband is filled.

---

5. Now cut out a decoration for the headband, and glue it on.

PURIM'S HERE AGAIN

Words and Music by Gail Kansky

Noi-sy greg-gars   Noi-sy Greg-gars
Hear the story   of Queen Es - ther

Ha-men-tas-chen   Ha-men-tas-chen
And her Un-cle   Mor-de-cai- i

Dres-sing up as Kings and Queens 'cause
Giv-ing gifts to those who need them

Pu - rim's here a - gain!
Pu - rim's here a - gain!

© Gail Kansky 1976

DANCE TO "PURIM'S HERE AGAIN"

1. Form circle. (Can also be done as a line dance.)

2. Join hands and take four hopping steps to right to first 8 notes.

    (Each hop takes two beats for a skipping hop.)

        a. right foot hop
           left foot hop

3. Repeat 2.

4. a. Step to right with right foot, bring left foot beside.

    b. Step right, kick across right with left foot.

    c. Back to left with left foot, bring right beside.

    d. Step left, kick across left with right foot.

5. Repeat starting with hop.

WHEN ESTHER WAS QUEEN

Words by Jay Englander
Music by Gail Kansky

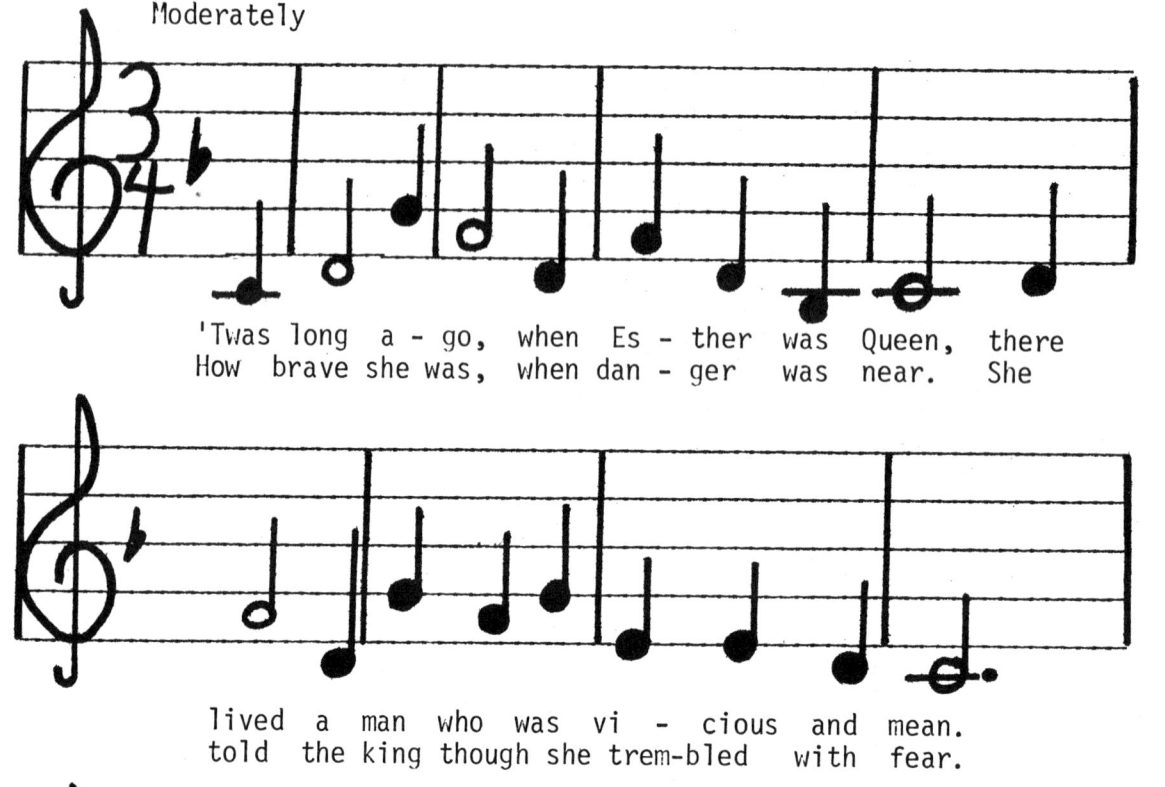

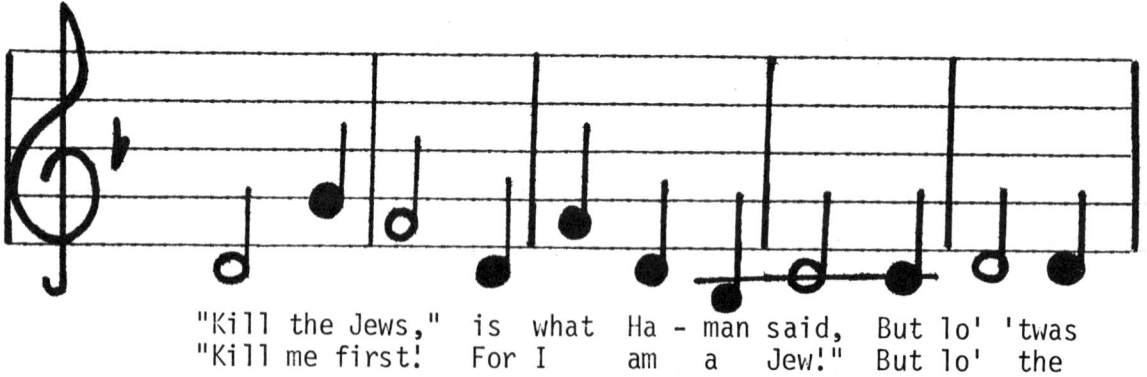

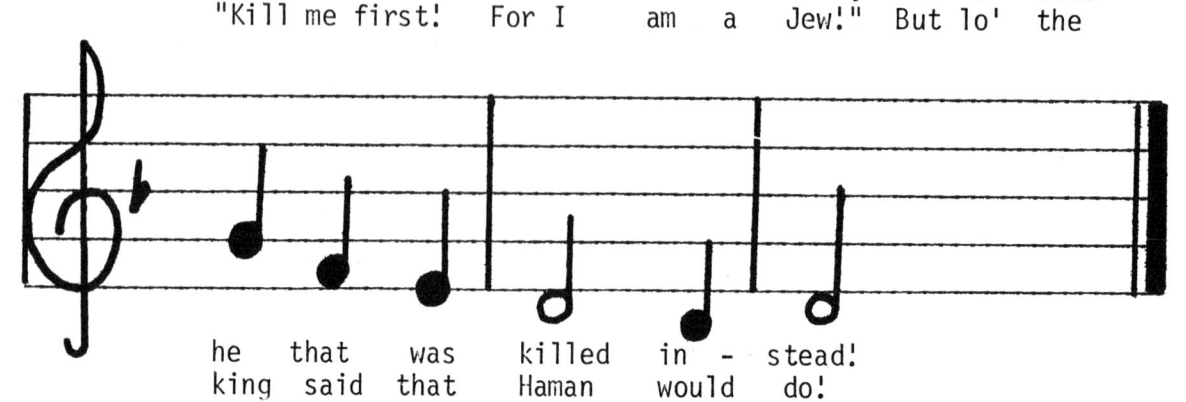

Moderately

'Twas long a-go, when Es-ther was Queen, there lived a man who was vi-cious and mean. "Kill the Jews," is what Ha-man said, But lo' 'twas he that was killed in-stead!

How brave she was, when dan-ger was near. She told the king though she trem-bled with fear. "Kill me first! For I am a Jew!" But lo' the king said that Haman would do!

@ Gail Kansky, Jay Englander 1976

PURIM DANCE

Music: Hag Purim" (see Additional Songs for Purim, page   )

This is a circle dance so form a nice round circle. Hold hands and count off by two's so that every person is either #1 or #2.

STEP I.   Six slides to the <u>right</u> starting with the right foot.

STEP II.   Three stamps in place - right, left, right.

STEP III. REPEAT Steps I and II to the left.

STEP IV.   ONLY #1's take one small leap into the center of circle and at the same time bend way down to a squatting position and hit the floor with your hands - right, left, right.

           ONLY #2's take one small leap backwards with your right foot. Then clap 3 times.

STEP V.   REVERSE Step IV (this time #1's go out and #2's go in.)

STEP VI.   REPEAT Step IV.

STEP VII. EVERYONE turns around in place. Now you're ready to begin again.

ADDITIONAL SONGS FOR PURIM

TITLE	SOURCES
"Purim Greeting"	SWS
"The King's Song"	SWS, NJSB, MSWS
"Mordecai's Procession"	SWS, NJSB, MSWS
"Yom Tov Lanu"	MSWS
"I Love the Day of Purim"	SWS
"Hag Purim"	SWS, NJSB, MSWS
"Esther In Your Garden"	SWS
"In Shu Shu Shushan"	SWS
"Esther"	SWS, NJSB, MSWS
"Mishak Purim"	MSWS
"Zemer L'Purim"	SWS, MSWS
"Ze Hayom"	SWS, MSWS
"Utzu Etza"	SWS, NJSB, MSWS
"For Purim"	SWS
"Shoshanat Ya'akov"	SWS, NJSB, MSWS
"Welcome to the Purim Fun"	PSP
"Play With Me, Dance With Me"	PSP
"Circle Round Together"	PSP
"Happy Purim"	PSP
"Esther, Esther"	PSP
"Purim Is A Holiday For You"	PSP

CAN YOU LISTEN?

Read a story of Haman. Every time Haman's name is said stamp your foot or clap your hands. Count how many times his name is read.

HAMANTASHEN

You will need:

   blackboard   paper
   pencils   chalk

The teacher writes the word "Hamantashen" on the board. The children must write down all the words they can find in that word.

                    Example: Hamantashen
                    Answer: man, as, tan, hen, an,
                                 hen, name, am, Haman,
                                 next, ten, hat

This game may be played with other words.

WHO AM I?

Think of a person. Name some of the deeds done by that person in Jewish history. The child who guesses the correct answer now has a turn to name the deeds of another person.

      Example: I helped save the Jews.
           I was a Queen.
           You think of men when it's Purim.
      Answer: Queen Esther

HAMAN ON THE GALLOWS

Children form a circle around a child (Haman) in the middle of that circle. The children sing:

   "Haman wants to get you

   Haman wants to get me

   Let's all look for Haman

   Ready, one, two, three."

When they sing the word "three", everyone sits down on the floor. The child in the center of the circle must try to tag one of the children before they are all sitting. If he succeeds, the child that's tagged goes to the center of the circle and becomes Haman. If he fails to tag a child, then he must be Haman again. The circle may reverse its walking direction at any time to avoid getting dizzy.

PIN THE CROWN ON ESTHER
or
PIN THE TAIL ON HAMAN'S HORSE

You will need:

    a piece of construction paper
    crayons
    scissors

    scarf
    tape (enough for each player to put on the back of his "tail" or "crown")

These games are played the same way as "Pin the Tail on the Donkey."

FIND THE GREGGAR

You will need:

    a greggar

One player leaves the room. Another player hides the greggar. The first player returns to the room and has to find the greggar. The only clues that can help him are the words "HAMAN" and "ESTHER." "HAMAN" means "You're far away from the hiding place." "ESTHER" means "you're close. Keep looking in this area."

HAMANTASHEN

You will need:

    1 c. butter
    2 c. sugar
    1 t. vanilla
jam

3 eggs
4 c. flour
1/2 t. salt

In a bowl, beat butter, sugar, eggs, and vanilla together. Add flour and salt. Mix well. This should make a stiff dough.

Roll dough flat with a rolling pin. Turn a glass upside down and press it down hard on the dough to cut out a circle.

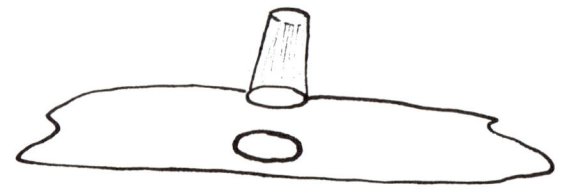

Fill each circle with a spoonful of jam.

Pinch the corners of the dough together to form a triangle. Put the Hamantashen on a well greased cookie sheet.

Set the oven to 350°.

Bake in the oven for 20 minutes or until golden brown.

SWEET AND SOUR MEATBALLS

You will need:

    1 jar chili sauce
    6 oz. grape jelly
    1 lb. hamburg

In a covered pot, mix the chili sauce and grape jelly. Bring to a boil.

Wet hands and shape hamburg into small balls. Put into the pot.

Cook on stove for 1 hour.

Serve over rice.

POTATO PUFFS

You will need:

    6 oz. box instant potatoes   4 c. water
    3 eggs   1 1/2 T. margarine
    1 1/2 t. salt   1 T. instant onions

Lightly grease a cupcake tin.

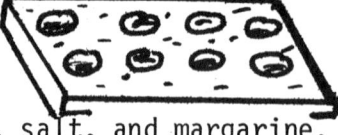

In a pot, boil water, salt, and margarine. Remove from heat. Add instant potatoes. Mix well.

Add eggs and onions, mix again. Spoon 2 tablespoons of mixture into each baking cup.

Set the oven to 450°.

Bake in the oven for 20 minutes or until golden brown.

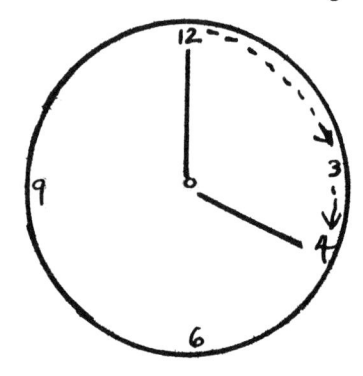

YUMMY FISH CHOWDER

You will need:

    1 lb. fish flounder
    1 small can mushrooms
    1 small can stewed tomatoes
    1 large onion

    4 c. water
    1 large can sliced potatoes
    1 large can sliced carrots

In a large covered pot, boil water. Lower heat to medium temperature.

Add all the ingredients to the pot.

Cook for 1 hour.

Serve hot with milk or plain.

TU B'SHVAT

PLANTER FOR SMALL TREE

You will need:

    plastic planter or ice cream holder
    white glue
    cord, raffia, macramé, twine, or rya rug twine

---

1. Apply a little glue to top of container. Wind cord around applying glue as you go. Different colors may be used to stripe background.

2. Decorate in a contrasting color with words or designs, gluing cord on as you go.

---

3. Plant your seedling tree for the Holiday inside your new planter.

Pre-School
Up

SPONGE PAINTING

You will need:

    1 piece of colored construction paper
    bits and pieces of sponges
    poster paint - 2 or 3 colors
    dishes for paint
    brown crayon or marker

---

1. Hold the paper the vertical way and draw a tree with branches but no leaves.

---

2. Dip sponges of different sizes and shapes into the various dishes of paint and blot onto the paper in various places on the branches. (To make the paint "stretch," dilute with water.)

MAKING TREES FROM DIFFERENT MEDIA

You will need:

Different materials depending upon the media selected

1. Melted Crayon Dropping Tree

    a. Cardboard is recommended. Draw a tree on the cardboard. Melt colored candles over tree. The drops will make the blossoms.

    b. The wax will adhere to the cardboard. No glue is necessary.

    c. A painted background is optional but nice.

2. Heavy Tempera Tree

    a. Paint a tree using the tempera paint very heavily to resemble a palette-knife oil painting.

    b. This can also be accomplished easily with acrylics.

3. Detergent Tree

    a. A crayon drawing of the tree trunk is first made.

    b. A bas-relief effect is achieved by using whipped detergent (water, detergent, and an egg beater) and coloring with two or more colors of food coloring.

4. Fold-Over Blotto Tree

    a. On the upper half of a paper, paint one side in a random design, fold the paper over to blot it on the other side.

    b. Using the blotted part as the foliage, draw (crayon) in the tree's trunk and outline the foliage.

5. Newspaper Palm Tree

    a. Cut the base of the palm tree from newspaper. Shred newspaper and glue on to form the fronds. A few circles of newspaper form the fruit.

    b. The background of sand, sea, mountain, etc. can be made from construction paper.

6. Gift Wrap Trees

    a. Flowering trees, drawn with a felt tip pen on gift wrap paper, may be cut out and mounted on contrasting colored paper.

POTATO INITIAL PRINT

You will need:

potato	paper
knife	carbon paper
pencil	paint
	small piece of felt

---

1. Place your paper over the carbon paper. Have the carbon shiny side up. Draw your Hebrew initial on the paper.

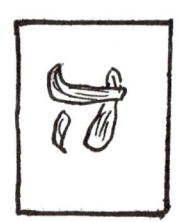

2. Now you will have your Hebrew initial in reverse on the other side of your paper. Cut your potato in half.

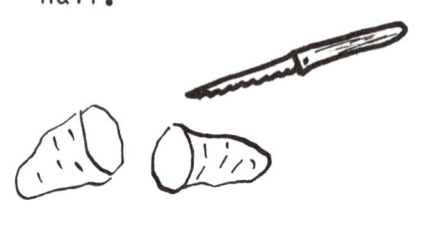

---

3. Now place your initial with the reverse letter up on the potato and press over the lines with a pencil.

4. With a sharp knife, very carefully cut away the background of the initial. Cut it down about 1/4 inch.

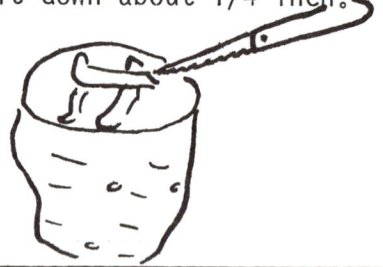

---

5. Now you are ready to print your Hebrew initial. You may want to make one large print, stationery, or you may have an idea of your own. Wet your piece of felt with paint, press the potato on the felt, and print away!

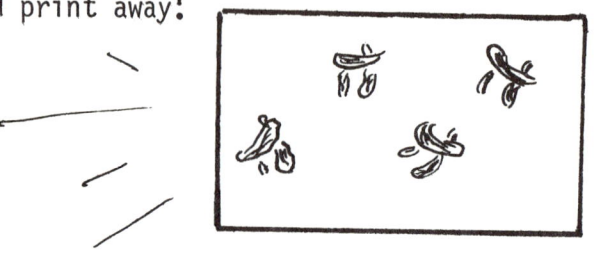

WEED AND TISSUE COLLAGE

You will need:

    weeds or grasses
    colored tissue paper
    cardboard or heavy construction paper

    white glue
    water
    clear plastic spray

---

1. Mix white glue and water in equal amounts. Brush mixture on cardboard.

2. While cardboard is still wet, add grasses or weeds to simulate trees.

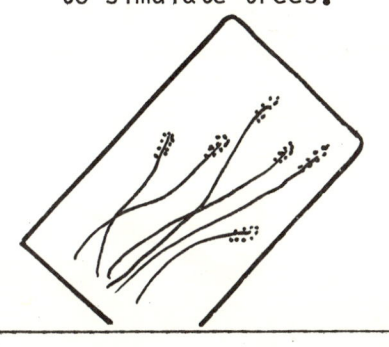

3. Now add bits of torn tissue paper over the weeds and brush each piece with glue-water mixture. Add more weeds and use brush with plenty of mixture to cover all.

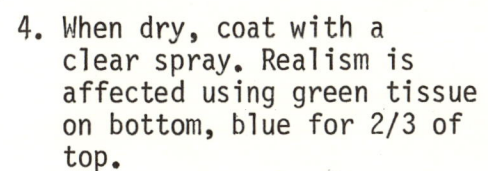

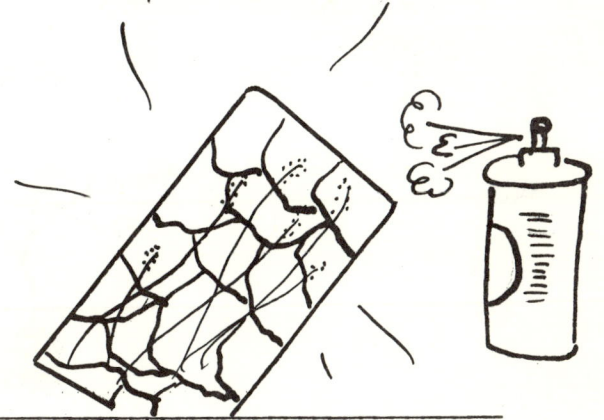

4. When dry, coat with a clear spray. Realism is affected using green tissue on bottom, blue for 2/3 of top.

BLOOMING ALMOND TREE

You will need:

    polystyrene beads
    stove and pot
    branch
    food can

    strong glue
    clay or other base
    spray paint, acrylics, or
        enamel

---

1. Paint can. When dry, put clay or other holder to secure branch to bottom of can.

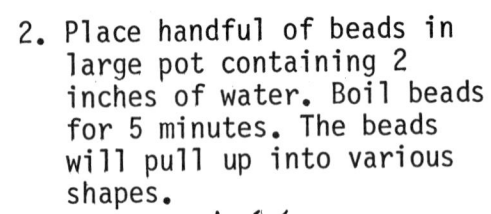

2. Place handful of beads in large pot containing 2 inches of water. Boil beads for 5 minutes. The beads will pull up into various shapes.

---

3. Apply coat of glue to small branch. Sprinkle the beads on pasted branch.

CAN NAPKIN RINGS

Easier napkin rings may be made with cardboard rolls from bathroom tissue. These can be either painted with water colors, felt tip pens, or crayons.

You will need:

    small food can
    paints (acrylic works best)

---

1. Remove bottom lid from can. Wash thoroughly.

2. Paint background one solid color. Let dry. (Acrylics dry very fast.)

3. Paint on design for holiday or Hebrew word.

4. When dry, insert rolled napkin.

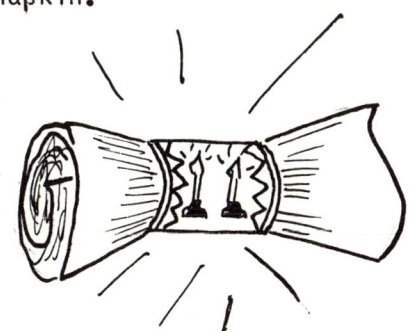

Pre-School
Up

FELT BEANBAGS

These may be made in the shape of a Hamantashen for Purim, the Ten Commandments for Shavuos, a dreidle for Chanukah, or the Star of David for Shabbat.

You will need:

    felt in various colors
    strong white glue
    funnel or paper to form one
    dry beans, rice, corn, or something similar
    scissors

1. Placing two felt squares one on top of the other, cut out your design. We are using Haman's face as an example.

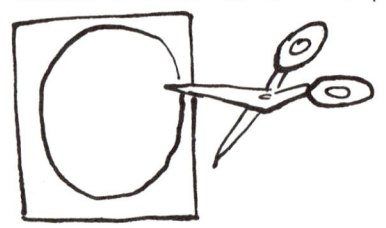

2. Cut out small pieces of felt to decorate your beanbag.

3. Glue the small felt pieces onto the larger felt design.

4. Glue the edges of the two large felt pieces together leaving a small opening.

5. When the glue is dry, pour in the beans or inside material. Use a funnel to do this. If you do not have a funnel, shape a piece of paper into a cone shape, glue together, and use that.

6. Now glue together your small opening and your beanbag is ready to play with!

TU B'SHVAT

Music by Jay Englander
Words by Gail Kansky

Allegro

Trees help to feed us and give us shade
We'll save our pen-nies, Send them a- way.

They're one of the best things that God ev - er
Mon - ey in Is- rael will plant my tree one

made -
day - : { We'll plant our own seed-lings for Tu B' -

Shvat. Then we'll grow as they grow each year - .

© Gail Kansky, Jay Englander, 1976

CREATIVE MOVEMENT FOR TU B'SHVAT

Music: "Tu B'Shvat" (p.   )

Pretend that you are a new seedling, planted in honor of the holiday of Tu B'Shvat. Start out on the floor, in a kneeling position, head bent down to the floor, arms crossed over your chest. As the song is sung, slowly rise up onto your knees, and unfold your arms. Try to pretend that you are growing, ever so slowly, into a strong tree. As the song ends you should be standing tall, waving your arms (branches) in the breeze.

NOTE: Some children can sing the song and others can pretend to be the gardener who wants the new seedling and takes good care of it as it grows.

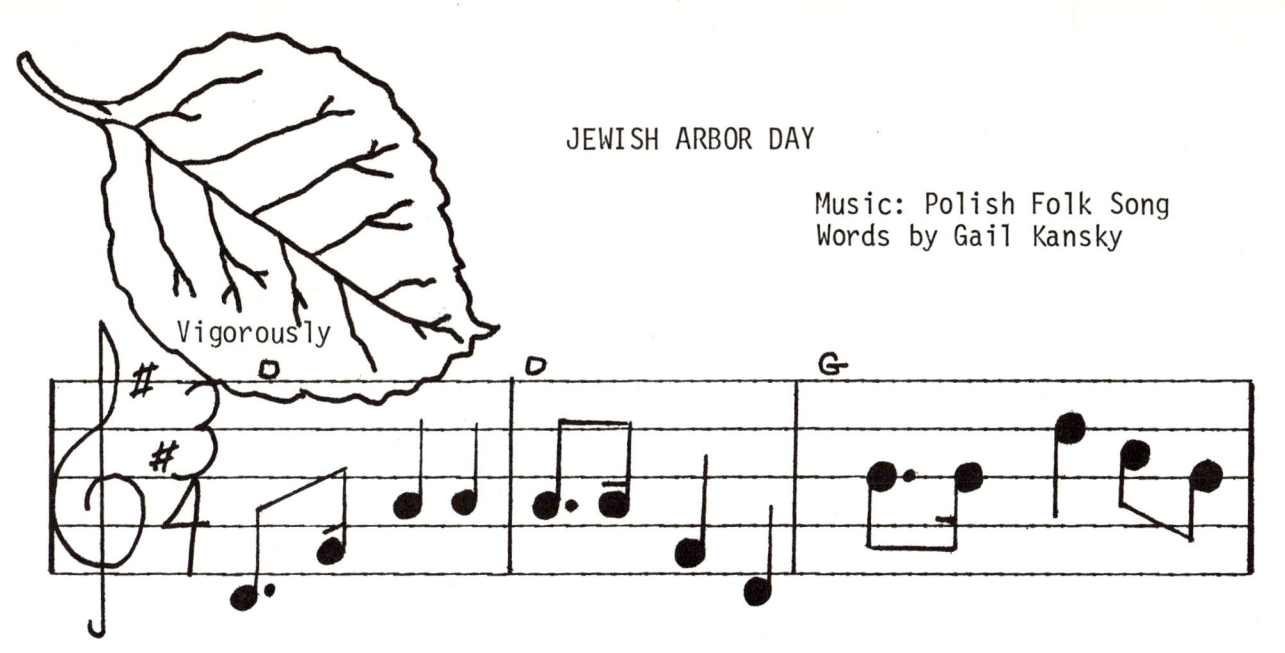

JEWISH ARBOR DAY

Music: Polish Folk Song
Words by Gail Kansky

Birds are crow-ing, ri-vers flow-ing, fields have fresh green grass grow-ing. Fields have fresh green grass grow-ing. Join our danc-ing, Plant a tree now. It's Jew-ish Ar-bor Day. Join our danc-ing, Plant a tree now, we are hap-py and gay!

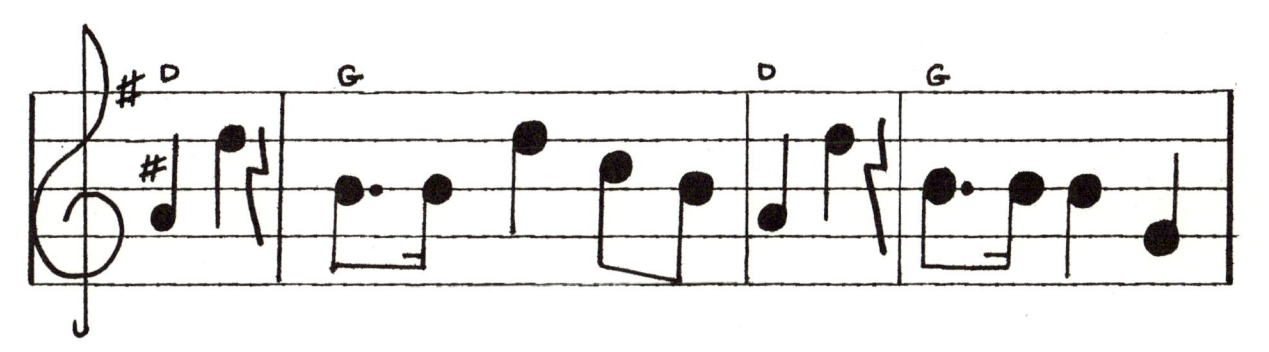

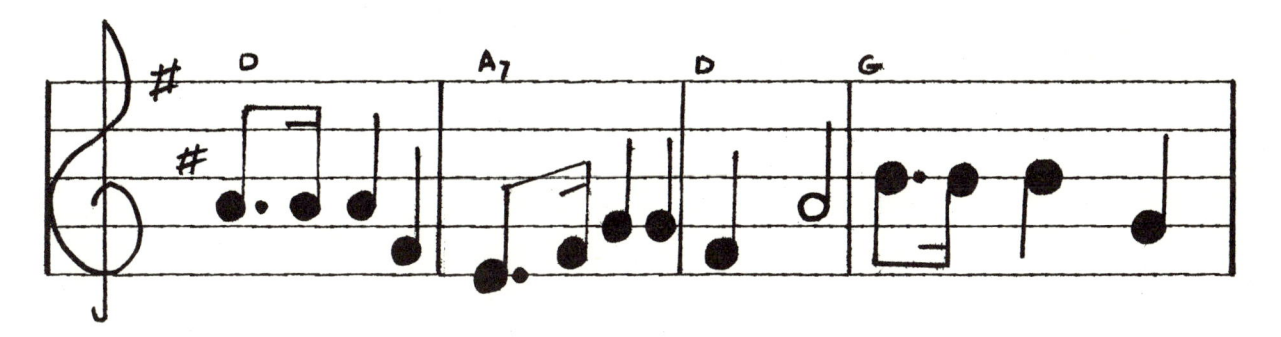

© Gail Kansky 1976

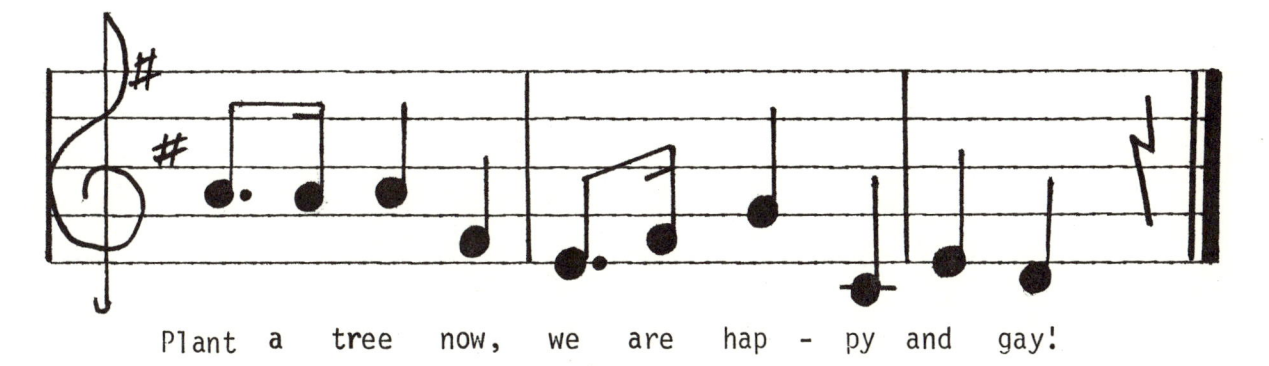

ADDITIONAL SONGS FOR TU B'SHVAT

TITLE	SOURCES
"Haskejyah"	NJSB, MSWS
"Kah Holhim Hashotlim"	SWS, MSWS
"Atzey Zetim Omdim"	SWS
"L'Shana Tova Shkediya"	SWS
"El Hasade"	SWS
"Ki Tavo'u"	SWS, MSWS
"Shir Hashatil"	SWS
"Shibolet Ba-sade"	NJSB
"Hag Etsim"	NJSB, MSWS

BLINTZE

Children sit in a circle. A player in the center tells a story about a person or object. Every time he comes to the object word he says "BLINTZE." The children must guess the "BLINTZE."

>Example: A BLINTZE hangs on my door.
>I kiss the BLINTZE when I leave
>or enter my house. Inside the
>BLINTZE are special words.

Answer: Mezzuzeh

BALL PASS

You will need:

ball

A child holds the ball and begins to tell a story. He throws the ball to another child who continues the story. This child in turn passes it to another child who adds to the story and so it continues. The stories should relate to a happening in Israel.

>Example: "It was a hot, dry day in Israel. (pass the ball) The next child continues: "The children sat around trying to guess who was coming for dinner." (pass the ball) The next child says: "Mother was busy in the kitchen preparing her favorite recipes." The ball pass game continues until every child has had a turn or the story is ended.

FRUIT TAG

Children make 2 circles, one near the other. A child in each circle is given the name of a fruit, as many fruits as there are children. In each circle there will be one apple, one pear, one banana, one date, one fig, one peach, one plum, and so on. One child remains outside the circle and is the caller. The caller says the name of a fruit, that fruit in each circle must take the place in the other fruit's circle. The caller must try to get into the place where the fruit stood before the fruit does. If he succeeds he becomes that fruit and the fruit becomes the caller.

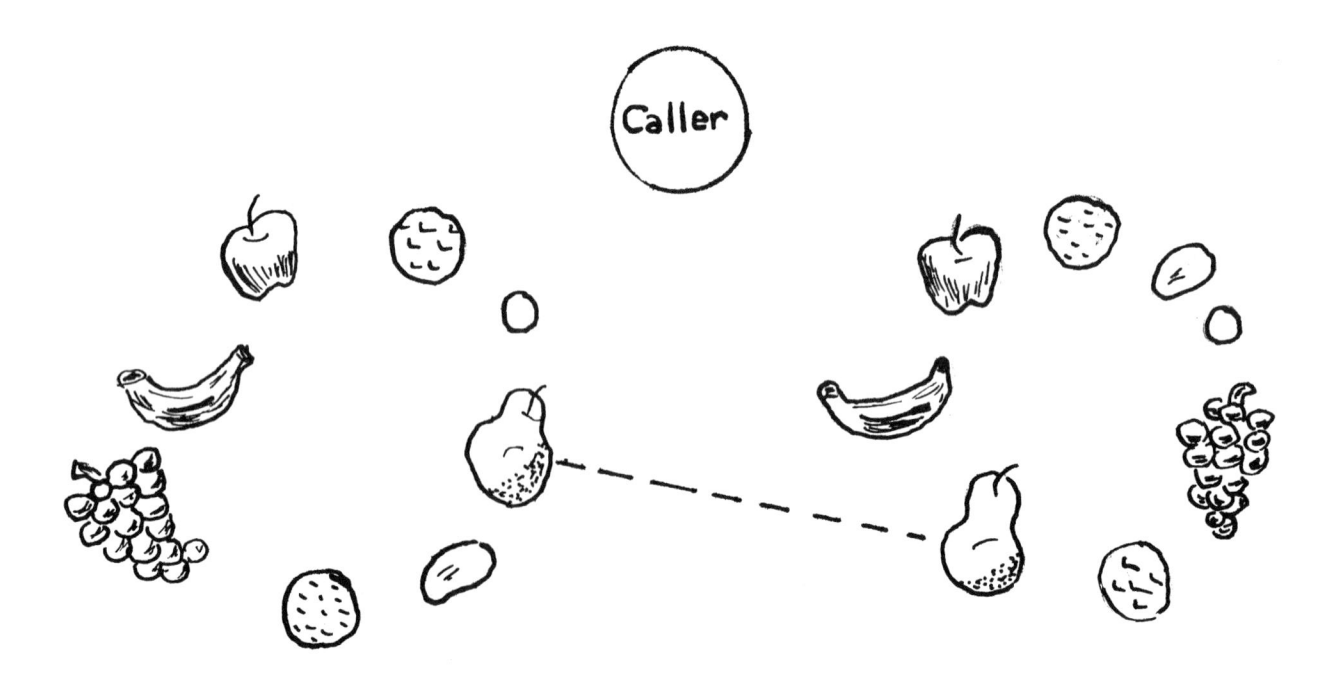

FIND ALEPH

You will need:

yardstick

Each child is given the name of a Hebrew letter. One child stands in the center of a circle holding a yardstick. That child calls out a Hebrew letter and lets the yard stick fall. The child who is that letter must catch the yard stick before it touches the ground. If the child is able to catch the stick he takes the place of the child in the center of the circle and may now call out another letter. If he does not catch the stick in time, the child in the center calls another letter.

COMMUNICATION

Children sit in a large circle. A player starts the game by whispering a sentence in another child's ear. That child in turn repeats the exact sentence to the next child and so on. The last child to receive the message must repeat it out loud. It is fun to hear how much the original sentence has changed as it was passed along.

FRENCH TOAST

You will need:

    4 slices of bread   1 T. milk
    2 eggs   1/2 t. salt
    1 T. butter

In a dish, mix 2 eggs, milk, and salt together.

Dip each slice of bread into the mixture. Do this on each side of the bread.

Melt butter in a pan on the stove. Set the temperature at Medium.

Put the bread in the pan until it browns. Turn it over with a spatula and brown on the other side.

Serve with apple sauce, sour cream, or maple syrup.

TEA SANDWICH

You will need:

    cream cheese   jam
    cookie cutters   peanut butter
    bread

On a cutting board, put a slice of bread, trim crust.

Take a cookie cutter and press down on the bread hard enough to cut out the shape.

With a knife, spread on some cream cheese, jam, or peanut butter.

Make as many sandwiches as you need.

Serve with a cold glass of milk.

GRAHAM SQUARE DELIGHTS

You will need:

    1 c. graham cracker crumbs   1 t. vanilla
    1 can condensed milk   6 oz. chocolate tidbits
                                           1 c. walnuts (optional)

Mix all the ingredients together in a bowl.

Lightly grease and flour an 8 inch baking pan. Pour the batter into the pan.

Set the oven to 350°.

Bake in the oven for 35 minutes.

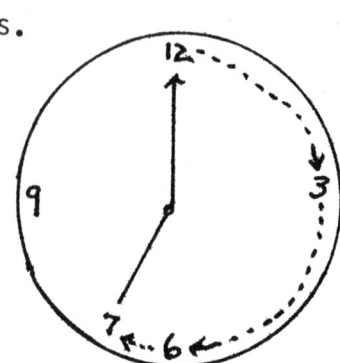

PASSOVER

Pre-School
Up

CAMERA-LESS PHOTOGRAPH

You will need:

    photography paper
    tray or heavy cardboard
    toothpicks (or other objects)
    fixative liquid (reusable)
    deep pan for fixative
    a sunny day

---

1. Place photography paper on tray and arrange toothpicks on paper to form star of David and design.

2. Go outside and, facing the sunny east, hold tray to receive direct sunlight.

   This part just takes minutes!

---

3. When the paper turns purple-y brownish, remove the toothpicks. Place paper in fixing liquid.

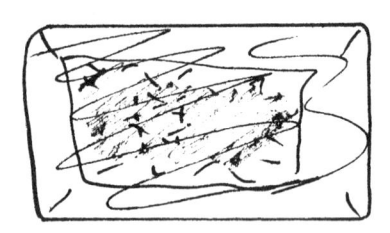

4. Hang your photo to dry!

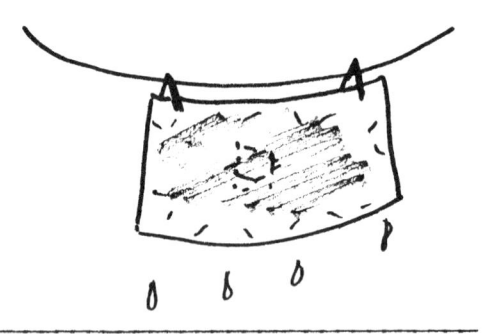

---

5. You may make your photograph a special greeting card or use just as decoration!

MATZAH HOLDER

You will need:

    2 c. salt
    4 c. flour
    2 c. water
    casserole dish 8" or larger

    rolling pin
    varnish
    vegetable oil

---

1. Mix salt and flour together. Add water slowly. Knead about 10 minutes until mixture is smooth.

2. Grease casserole dish. Using rolling pin, roll mixture about 1/4 inch thick. Cut into four one inch strips. Lay strips inside dish crriss-crossing them.

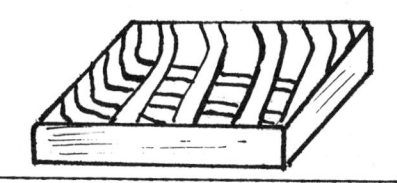

3. With excess dough mix, divide in half and roll with palm of hand into breadstick shape pieces. Twist them together and form rim on dish. Moisten the parts that touch with water to bind them.

4. Bake in a 325° oven until light brown (about 1 hour and 30 min.) Or, let air dry for a full two days on a window screen.

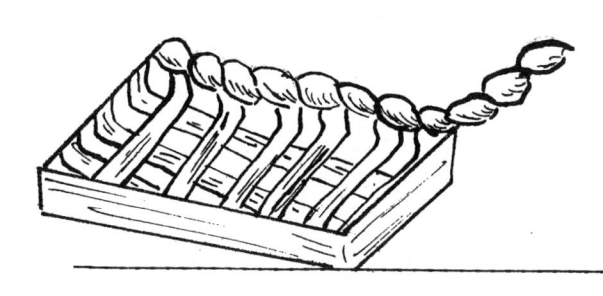

5. When cool, varnish holder to protect it from moisture. After using holder, clean with damp cloth or sponge.

WOVEN PLACEMATS

You will need:

    2 pieces of construction paper
       (pick colors that you like together)
    scissors
    stapler

---

1. Hold one piece of paper lengthwise and fold it in half.

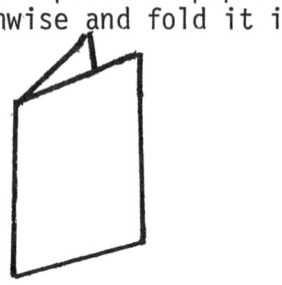

2. Start at the folded edge and cut slits all the way across but stop one inch away from the outer edge. Space your cuts evenly.

---

3. Cut your second piece of paper into long, narrow strips.

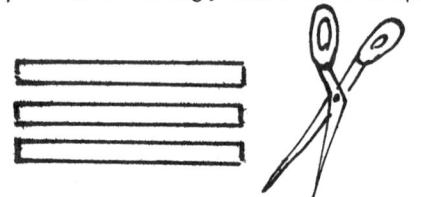

4. Open the first piece of paper and lie it flat on the table.

---

5. Take one strip and "weave" it over and under the slits. Do the same with all of your strips. NOTE: If your first strip was woven <u>over</u> first and then <u>under</u>, make the second strip start <u>under</u> first. Secure ends with stapler.

You can "weave" placemats for everyone at your holiday table.

136

PASSOVER WINE COASTERS

You will need:

    yarn   scissors
    pieces of thick cardboard or cork   white shellac
    white glue   pencil

---

1. Draw a bunch of grapes or bottle of wine on the cardboard or cork. Cut it out carefully.

---

2. Spread glue on small section of outline and fill in with yarn, starting in the middle and winding it around. Press yarn down firmly.

---

3. When glue is dry on yarn, give coaster three or four thin coats of shellac. Let dry between each coat.

MATZAH COVER

You will need:

    a square of cloth   brown paper
    crayons   iron
    liquid starch   common pin

---

1. Decorate a square of cloth with wax crayons.

2. Sprinkle liquid starch on cloth, then iron on hot setting between two pieces of brown paper.

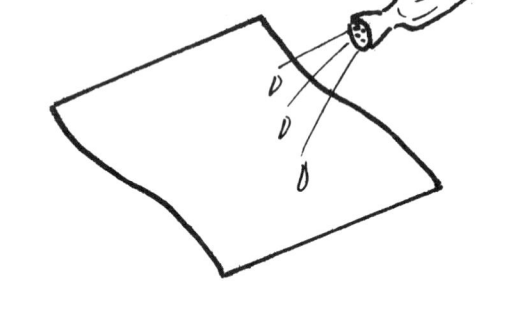

---

3. (Optional) Fringe ends separating threads one by one with common pin.

Pre-School
Up

WINDOW ORNAMENT

You will need:

    a clear plastic cover from a container of any size
    tiny plastic chips in at least two different colors
        (fish bowl or plant chips are good)
    strong glue
    needle
    thread

---

1. Decide upon a design or symbol of the holiday you are going to use.

2. Using the needle, punch a hole near the edge of the cover.

3. Spread glue evenly over surface.

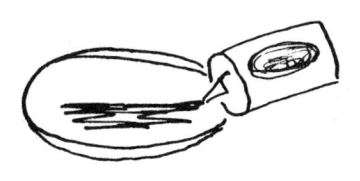

4. Arrange plastic chips in the design you choose.

---

5. After allowing glue to dry, pull a thread through the needle hole and knot to use as a hanger.

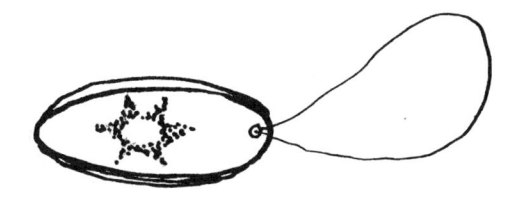

6. Hang your window ornament in a window and let the sun shine through to make it sparkle!

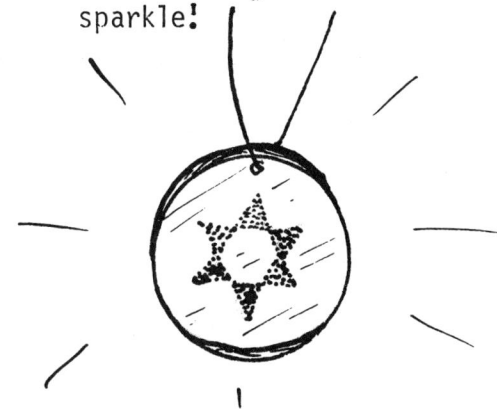

Pre-School Up

HEBREW PLAQUE

You will need:

   toothpicks (if child is young, substitute popsicle sticks)
   cardboard
   felt (enough to cover cardboard)
   paint (felt-tip pens may be used instead of paint)
   glue

---

1. Glue felt on cardboard for background.

2. Paint toothpicks two colors (less or more colors optional).

---

3. Paste toothpicks on felt to form a Hebrew word such as Shalom, Mazel, Chai, Pesach, etc. Make Hebrew letters as shown below.

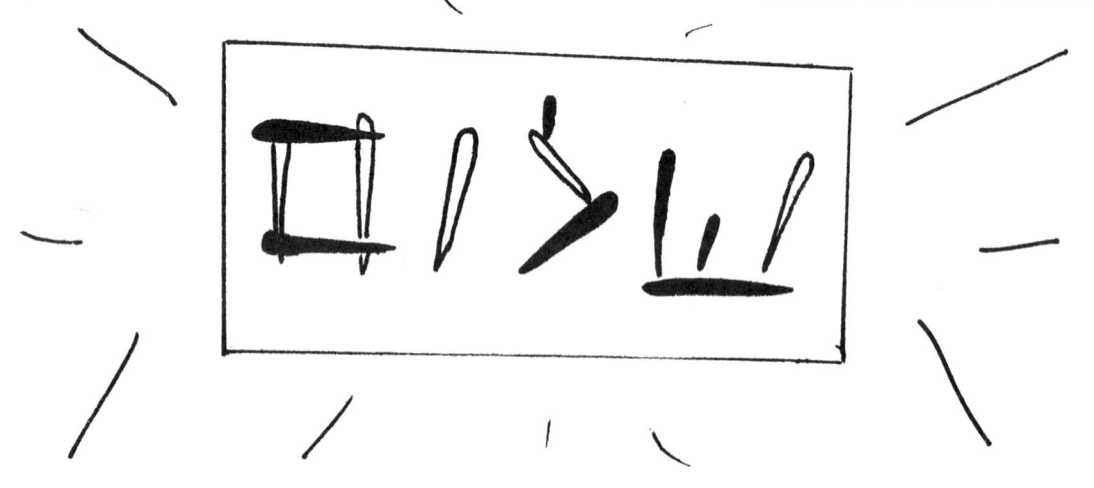

140

AFIKOMEN BAG

You will need:

    two men's handkerchiefs   iron
    crayons   needle and thread
    paper (brown is best)

---

1. Decorate one handkerchief with crayons. Make a nice Passover scene or design.

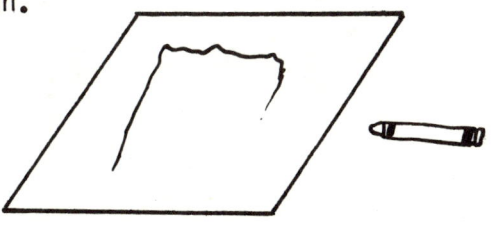

---

2. Put the handkerchief in the middle of two pieces of paper and set the picture with a warm iron.

---

3. With the design side facing in, sew three sides of the handkerchiefs together about 1/2 inch in from the edge or less.

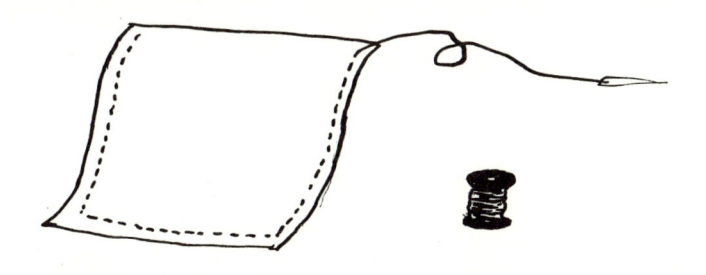

---

4. Now turn the design side right side out and place on the Sedar table for Father to hide the Afikomen in. Mother will like not having matzos crums around.

THE SEDER

Music by Jay Englander
Words by Gail Kansky

Gaily

Wel-come to our Pass-o-ver Se - der.

Why is this night diff'- rent?

Af-i-ko-men's hid - den. Find it!

Now we'll end the Se - der!

© Gail Kansky, Jay Englander 1976

WHO DID?

Unknown Author
Lyrics by Gail Kansky

Lively

Who did? Who did? Who did? Who did?
Pha-roah's daugh-ter, Pha-roah's daugh-ter
Who did? Who did? Who did? Who did?
Pha-roah, Pha-roah, Pha-roah, Pha-roah
Who did? Who did? Who did? Who did?
God did. God did. God did. God did.

Who did find the ba-by Mo-ses?
Pha-roah's daugh-ter found the baby.
Who did bad things to the He-brews?
Pha-roah did the ve-ry bad things.
Who did bring the plagues on Pha-roah?
God did bring the plagues on Pha-roah.

143

Who did? Who did? Who did? Who did?
Pha - roah's daugh - ter, Pha - roah's daugh - ter,
Who did? Who did? Who did? Who did?
Pha - roah, Pha - roah, Pha - roah, Pha - roah,
God did. God did. God did. God did.

Who did find the bas - ket float - ing?
Pha - roah's daugh - ter found the ba - by.
Who did make them slaves in Eg - ypt?
Pha - roah made the He - brews be slaves.
Who did bring the plagues on Pha - roah?
God did bring the plagues on Pha - roah.

Who did? Who did? Who did? Who did?
Pha - roah's daugh - ter, Pha - roah's daugh - ter
Who did? Who did? Who did? Who did?
Pha - roah, Pha - roah, Pha - roah, Pha - roah,
Who did? Who did? Who did? Who did?
God did. God did. God did. God did.

Who did find the ba - by Mo - ses?
Pha - roah's daugh - ter found the ba - by.
Who did bad things to the He-brews?
Pha - roah did the ve - ry bad things.
Who did bring the plagues on Pha-roah?
God did bring the plagues on Pha-roah.

Who did see the bas-ket? Who did find the ba-by?
She did see the bas-ket. She did find the ba-by.
Who was ve - ry wick-ed? Who was ve - ry cru - el?
He was ve - ry wick-ed. He was ve - ry cru - el.
Who was ve - ry an - gry? Who did bring the ten plagues?
God was ve - ry an - gry. God did bring the ten plagues.

Who took ba - by Mo - ses home?
She took ba - by Mo - ses home.
Who would not let the Jews go?
He would not let the Jews go.
Who helped Mo - ses free the Jews?
God helped Mo - ses free the Jews.

© Gail Kansky 1976

ADDITIONAL SONGS FOR PASSOVER

TITLE	SOURCE
"Ma Nishtana"	NJSB
"Avodim Hoyinu"	SWS, MSWS
"V'hi She'omdo"	SWS, NJSB
"Haleluyoh"	SWS, NJSB, MSWS
"Eliyohu Hanovi"	SWS, NJSB
"Adir Bimluho"	SWS, NJSB, MSWS
"L'Shono Habo'o"	SWS
"Ehod Mi Yodea"	SWS, NJSB, MSWS
"Had Gadyo"	SWS, NJSB, MSWS
"Concerning a Kid"	SWS, NJSB
"Ha Lahma"	NJSB
"The Ballad of the 4 Sons"	MSWS
"Four Sons Are We"	SSA
"I'd Be Happy"	SSA
"Freedom Song"	SSA
"Will Elijah Visit Me?"	SSA
"The Singing Seder Table"	SSA

PHAROAH'S HOP

You will need:

   chalk

Draw a large X on the floor. Children form a line at one end of the X. Holding the left leg with the left hand the child hops down one side of the X. Holding the right leg with the right hand he hops back up the other side of the X. If his leg touches the ground, he must go to the end of the line and start over again.

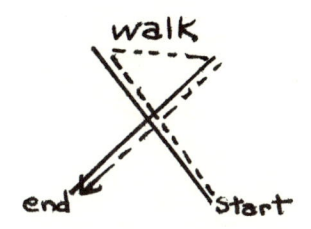

CROSSING THE RED SEA

You will need:

   chalk

Draw 2 lines about 3 feet apart. Children line up behind one line and try to jump over to the other line. If he touches the "Red Sea" between the lines, he must go to the end of the line and try to cross over again.

WHERE'S THE AFIKOMEN?

The children form 2 circles, one inside the other. One circle should have an even number of children, the other one an uneven number. The extra child in the circle is the caller. The children march around until the caller says "afikomen." The children quickly drop hands and find a partner. The child who is left without a partner is the afikomen and becomes the caller, and the old caller takes the extra child's place.

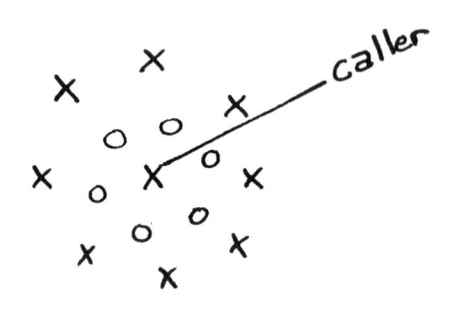

COMPOTE

You will need:

    chalk

Draw a line. Children stand at opposite ends of the line. One player stands in the center of the line. The children at the ends of the line recite:

> "I am an apple
> I fell from the tree
> If you want a bite
> Try and catch me."

With that, the children try to exchange places without being tagged by the child in the middle.

CHAROSES

You will need:

    1 apple sliced fine   1/2 c. nuts chopped
    1/2 t. cinnamon   2 T. red wine

In a bowl, mix the apple, wine, nuts, and cinnamon until mixture is smooth.

Put in a small dish for the Seder plate.

FRIED MATZOS

You will need:

    2 pieces of Matzos   1/2 t. salt
    1 c. water   2 eggs

Break matzos into small pieces. Put in a bowl.

Boil water and pour it over the matzo. Add eggs and salt. Mix well.

Heat a pan on the stove with butter or oil. Lower to medium temperature and pour batter into pan.

Cook until golden brown. Turn and brown other side.

Serve with apple sauce or sour cream.

PASSOVER ROLLS

You will need:

    1/2 c. water   1/2 c. oil
    1/2 T. sugar   1/4 t. salt
    1 c. matzo meal   2 eggs

In a pot, boil water and oil.

In a bowl, mix matzo meal, salt, and sugar together. Pour the oil mixture over it. Add eggs, one at a time, and mix well. Let stand 15 minutes.

Set the oven to 375°.

Bake in the oven for 40 minutes or until golden brown.

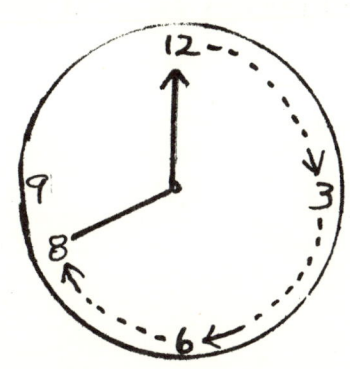

MACAROONS

You will need:

    2 egg whites   1/2 t. lemon juice
    1/2 c. powdered sugar   hand mixer
    4 oz. shredded coconut   cookie sheet

Using the hand mixer, beat egg whites until they are stiff. (They will stand up in peaks.)

Add sugar, lemon juice and blend. Add shredded coconut and mix well.

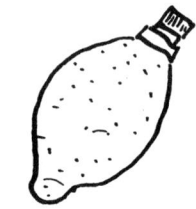

Drop by spoonful onto a lightly greased cookie sheet.

Set oven at 275°.

Bake for about 30 minutes or until golden brown.

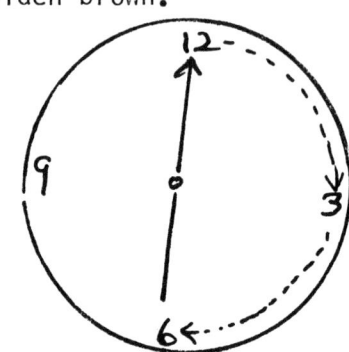

FESTIVE GEFILTE FISH

You will need:

    1 large jar of Gefilte Fish
    lettuce leaves, washed and drained
    small jar of red horseradish
    small jar of sliced cooked carrots

On each plate (salad or dessert size) place one or two lettuce leaves.

Place 2 pieces of gefilte fish on the bed of lettuce.

Put a teaspoon of horseradish on one side of the fish and 2 or 3 slices of carrot on the other.

BAKED FISH

You will need:

    1 lb. of fish flounder   1 or 2 eggs
    1/2 t. salt
    1/2 c. matzo meal

In a dish mix the salt and egg.

Wash the fish clean and dip into the egg mixture.

In another dish measure out the matzo meal, dip the fish into the mixture. Be sure to coat both sides.

Put the fish in a shallow pan.

Set the oven to 350°.

Bake in the oven 20 minutes or until flaky.

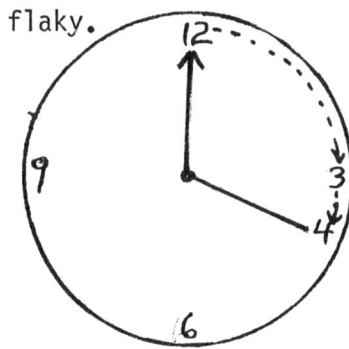

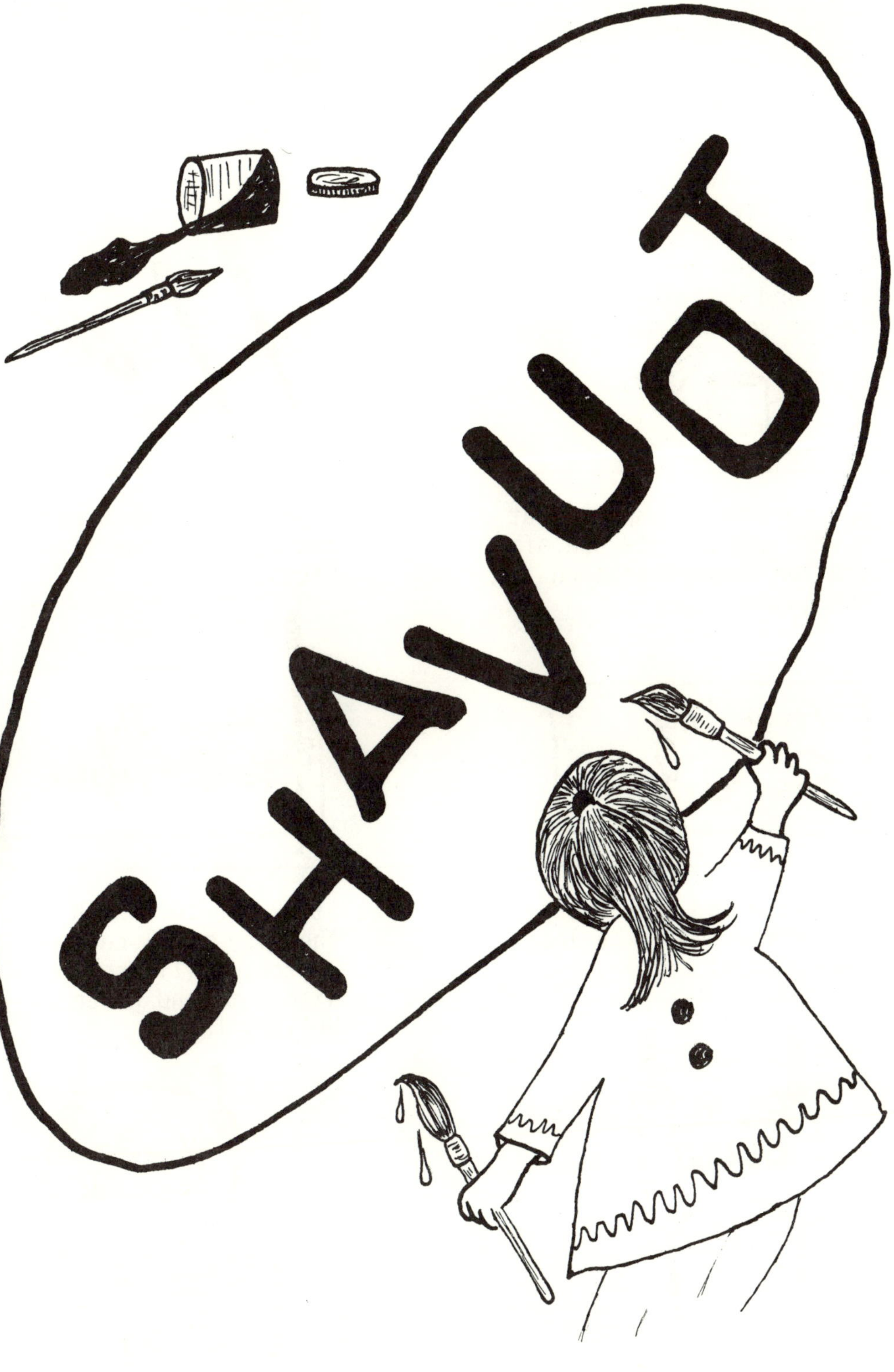
SHAVUOT

SHAVUOT NUT CUP

You will need:

- cover of a spray can
- aluminum foil
- clay or florist's clay
- scissors
- toothpicks
- crayons or felt tip pens
- tape or glue
- paper

---

1. Place a bit of clay on the bottom inside of the can cover. Then cover the entire cap with foil by setting the top on the foil and wrapping the ends inside so they don't show.

2. Color two toothpicks black.

---

3. Cut a strip of paper about 1 1/2" x 5". Write one of the Ten Commandments on the paper.

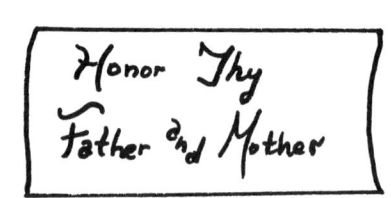

4. Tape or glue each end of the paper to the toothpicks.

---

5. Roll each end of the paper toward the center to look like a small scroll.

6. Stick one toothpick into the clay (foil covered) bottom. Fill the cup with nuts and place on your holiday table.

Pre-School
Up

PARTY STRAWS

You will need:

paper   scissors
crayon   straw

---

1. Cut paper in shape of decoration for holiday. Then color.

2. Cut two holes in paper decoration. Slip the straw through both holes. Make some for your friends!

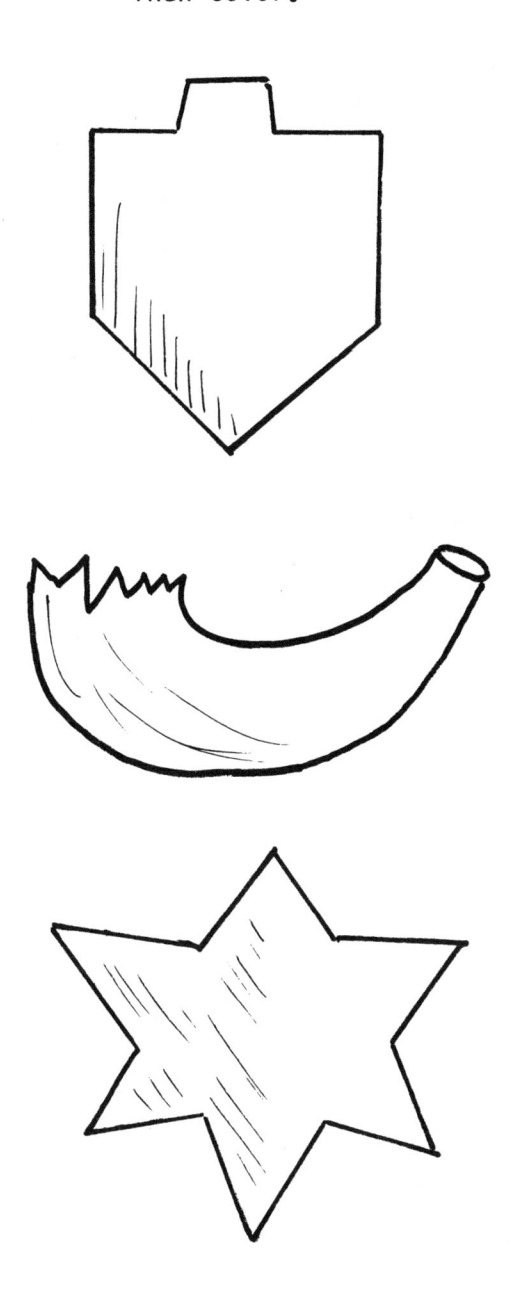

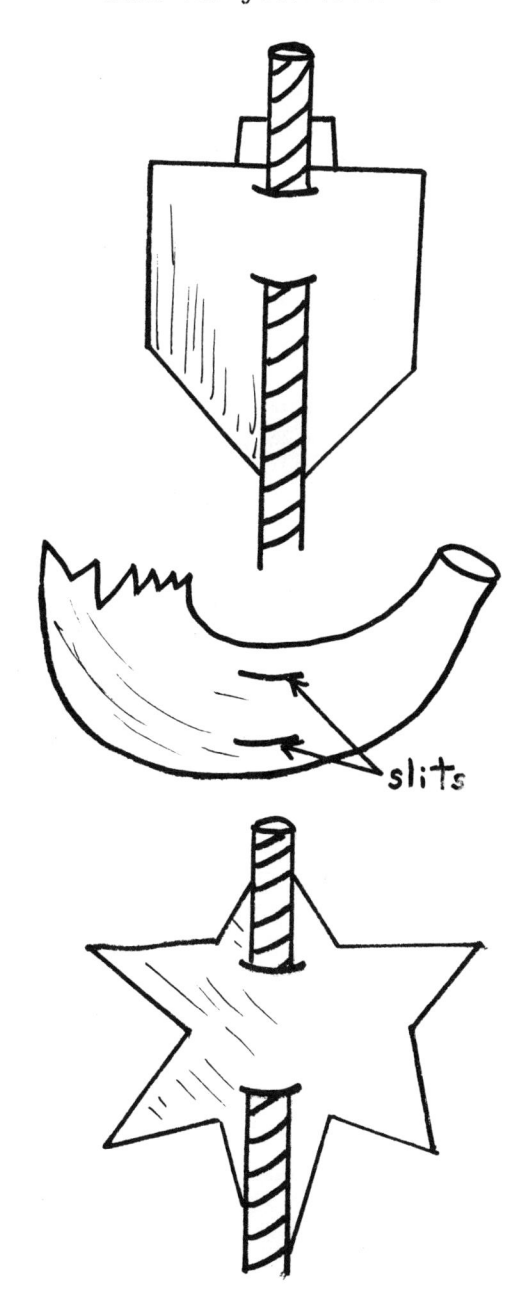

slits

157

Pre-School
Up

YOUR OWN MEZUZAH

You will need:

    small box (matchbox or similar)   colored paper
    paper   aluminum foil
    pen   glue
        scissors

---

1. Print the "Shema" on a piece of paper and put it into the box.

---

2. Cover the closed box with aluminum foil.

---

3. Glue on some pretty decorations.

---

4. You may use some inverted tape to hang it "upon the doorposts" of your very own bedroom!

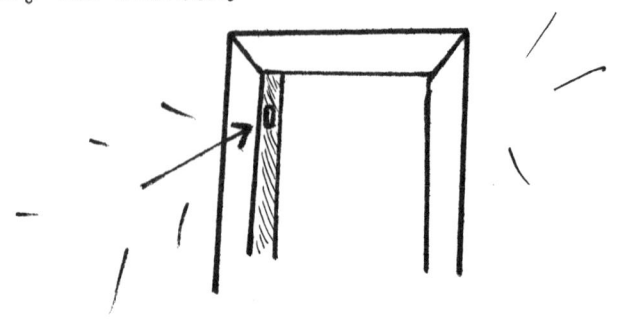

158

TEN COMMANDMENT PLAQUE

You will need:

    heavy cardboard (may be cut from a carton)
    paper-maché mixture (the recipe is found under the Yom Tov Nut Cup)
    silver or gold paint
    one color contrasting color paint
    paint brushes (one thin for lettering)

---

1. Cut your piece of cardboard in the shape of the tablets shown below.

2. Put paper-maché around the edges of the tablets to form a border. (You may paste various shaped noodles around instead of maché.)

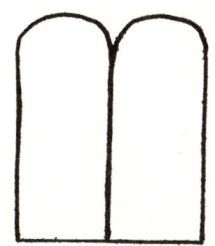

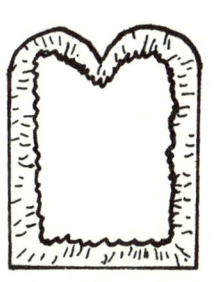

---

3. After paper-maché is dry, paint the entire surface with gold or silver paint.

4. When background paint is dry, add letters of the Ten Commandments to the tablets.

Pre-School
Up

FRAMED FINGER PAINTING

You will need:

    finger paints (a homemade recipe for this is below)
    paper for painting
    water
    scissors
    black or dark construction paper
    pencil

---

1. Soak your glazed painting paper with water, then lie flat on table.

2. Smooth globs of paint over entire surface of paper. Use your fingers, fingernails, fist, palm, etc. for different effects.

HOMEMADE FINGER PAINT: Mix 1 c. sugar, 1 c. water together. Pour 3 c. boiling water into top of double boiler and add mix. Stir and cook until thick. Remove from stove and add 1 T. boric acid and several drops oil of cloves. Divide into separate containers and add powdered paint for color.

3. Allow to dry flat on newspaper.

4. Draw an outline of a Torah or the Ten Commandment Tablets on the construction paper.

5. Cut out the center of the outline.

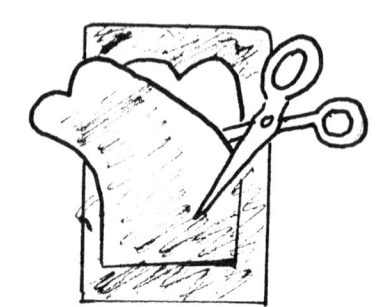

6. Paste the outside paper from which the design was cut over the finger painting.

Pre-School
Up

SELF-FRAME PICTURE

You will need:

    2 paper plates
    paste
    crepe paper streamers

    shellac
    2 gummed loose-leaf paper reinforcement circles

1. Paste the two paper plates back to back.

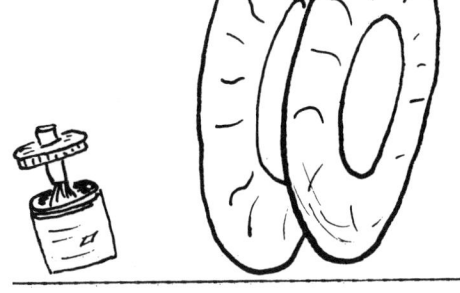

2. All around the edge of one plate glue a border of crepe paper.

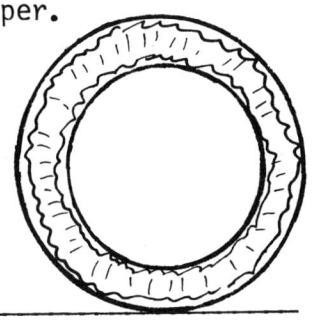

3. In the center of that same plate, glue on crepe paper making a pretty design for the holiday. Do not use too much of that paste!

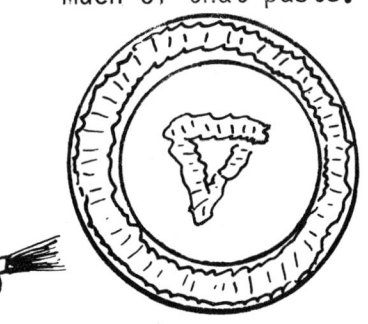

4. Spread a coat of clear shellac on your picture to make it shine.

5. Using the two gummed reinforcement circles, paste them back to back on the edge of the untrimmed plate for a hanger.

MINIATURE TORAH

You will need:

    paper (a long, narrow piece)
    2 popsicle sticks
    paste
    crayons
    a small piece of ribbon or yarn
    a small piece of fabric for the "mantel"

---

1. Draw pictures on your "scroll" of paper. Examples are: scenes showing the Ten Commandments, Noah's Ark, Bible stories.

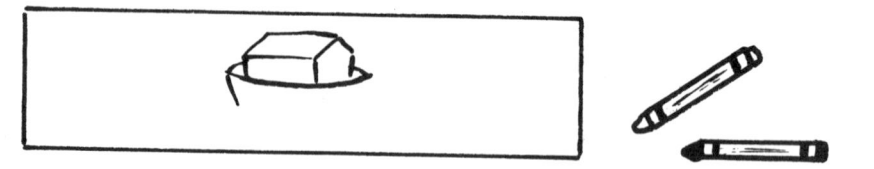

---

2. Make a line of paste up and down each end of your scroll and paste a popsicle stick on each end.

---

3. When the paste is dry, roll your Torah in from each end and tie it with the ribbon or yarn.

---

4. Cut the piece of fabric so it just fits around your Torah. Paste the two ends together. This forms the Torah Mantel.

SHAVUOT SONG

Music by Jay Englander
Words by Gail Kansky

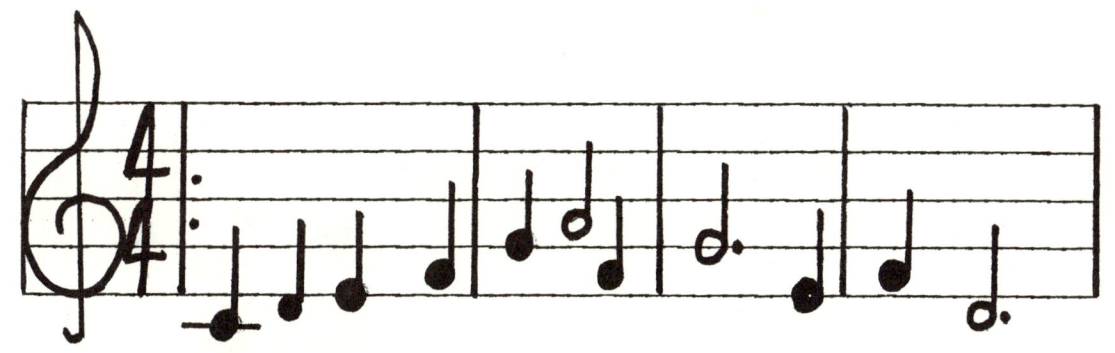

Cel-e-brate Sha-vu-ot with fruit and flow-ers
Gath-er-ing the fruit for the Har-vest sea-son

Jui-cy tas-ty fruit grew with sun and show-ers.
Ten Com-mand-ments gives us just one more rea-son.

© Gail Kansky, Jay Englander 1976

TORAT EMET

Traditional Hebrew Song
Arranged by Gail Kansky

Fairly Slow

To - rat e - met - na - tan l'amo El -

Al yad n' - vi - o - ne - man bey - to.

Lo ya - ha - lif - ha - . El v' lo ya - mir da -to.

Lo' - la - mim - , l'o - la - mim l' - zu - la to.

© Gail Kansky 1976

ADDITIONAL SONGS FOR SHAVUOT

TITLE	SOURCE
"To Fetch the Torah Down"	SWS, NJSB
"Shavuot Hymn"	SWS, MSWS
"Bikurim Lirushalayim"	SWS
"Heroes of the Law"	SWS
"Salenu"	SWS, NJSB
"Torah Lanu"	SWS, MSWS
"Kumu V'na'ale"	SWS
"Boruch Elohenu"	SWS, MSWS, NJSB
"Torat Emet"	SWS, MSWS, NJSB
"Yisrael V'oraita"	NJSB
"The Pilgrimage"	SWS
"Zemer Hag"	SWS
"Na'ale L'har Tsion"	MSWS
"Havu Godel"	MSWS

WHO DO?

Children form 2 lines, one behind the other. One child is the leader and faces the lines. He says "touch your toes" and each person follows what he does. He says "touch your nose" and touches his toes. The children who touch their nose must go to the back line. The children who touched their toes as the leader did come forward to the front line. You must do what the leader does, not what he says.

CATCH GOLIATH

Children make a circle around the child in the center, call him David. "David" must stand with his hand on his hip. The other children may approach him and say, "David, David, here I am...Catch me, catch me, if you can." David must try to tag the child without taking his hand off his hip or before the child returns to his place in the circle. If David tags the child, that child then becomes David and goes to the center of the circle.

SHAMOS

Children stand on one side of the room. The caller stands in the middle of the room. The caller says words that are familiar with a holiday and includes the word "Shamos." The children clap when the right word is called, and run to the other side of the room every time the word "Shamos" is called. When the children run to the other side of the room, the caller must try to tag one of the children out. That child then becomes the caller.

      Example: The Holiday is Chanukah.

                 The words may be

- Menorah - clap
- candle - clap
- Antiochus - clap
- present - clap
- Shamos - run, run, run...

QUICK BEET BORSHT

You will need:

    1 can sliced beets   1/3 c. lemon juice
    4 1/2 c. water   3 T. sugar
    1 large onion   1/2 t. salt

In a covered pot, place all the ingredients and bring to a boil.

Lower the heat to medium temperature.

Cook for 10 minutes. Remove from stove.

Remove onion and let cool.

Serve cold with sour cream or boiled potato.

MOCK PIZZA

You will need:

    4 slices of bread
    4 slices of cheese
    ketchup or slice of tomato

On a cookie sheet, place 4 slices of bread.

On each slice of bread, place a piece of cheese.

Pour a tablespoon of ketchup on the cheese or a slice of tomato.

Set the oven to 375°.

Bake in the oven for 15 minutes or until cheese melts.

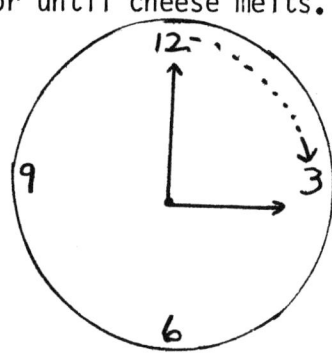

NOODLE CHEESE PUDDING

You will need:

    12 oz. noodles, cooked   1/2 t. salt
    1 pint sour cream   1/2 t. pepper
    1 lb. cottage cheese   1/2 c. sugar
    3 eggs   1/4 lb. butter

In a bowl, mix all of the above ingredients.

Pour into a well greased 9 x 13 inch pan.

Set the oven to 350°.

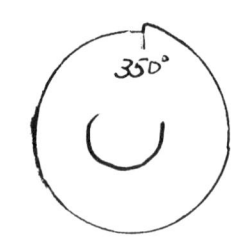

Bake in the oven for 1 hour or until golden brown.

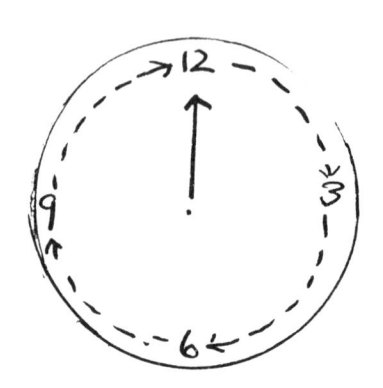

PINEAPPLE SURPRISE SALAD

You will need:

    4 lettuce leaves, washed
    1 small can pineapple rings
    8 oz. cottage cheese
    1 jar cherries drained

On a plate, put a lettuce leaf.

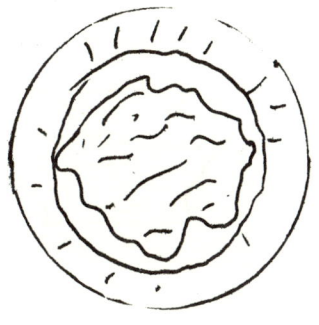

On the leaf, place a pineapple ring.

In the center of the pineapple, put a scoop or large tablespoon of cottage cheese.

Place a cherry in the center of the cottage cheese.

Yummy!

LIME MOLD

You will need:

    2 packages lime flavored Kosher gelatin
    3 c. water
    1/2 pt. sour cream
    1 small can crushed pineapple

In a bowl, dissolve the lime gelatin in 3 cups of boiled water.

Let cool for 10 minutes.

Mix in the sour cream and crushed pineapple.

Place in mold and refrigerate.

Serve when chilled.